CULTURE SMART!

CHINA

THE ESSENTIAL GUIDE TO
CUSTOMS & CULTURE

INDRE BALCIKONYTE-HUANG
AND KATHY FLOWER

KUPERARD

"The real voyage of discovery consists not in seeking new landscapes, but in having new eyes."

Adapted from Marcel Proust, *Remembrance of Things Past.*

ISBN 978 1 78702 880 7

British Library Cataloguing in Publication Data
A CIP catalogue entry for this book is available
from the British Library

First published in Great Britain
by Kuperard, an imprint of Bravo Ltd
59 Hutton Grove, London N12 8DS
Tel: +44 (0) 20 8446 2440
www.culturesmart.co.uk
Inquiries: publicity@kuperard.co.uk

Design Bobby Birchall
Printed in Turkey

ABOUT THE AUTHORS

INDRE BALCIKONYTE-HUANG was born in Vilnius, Lithuania. She has a Bachelor's degree in Chinese with Economics from the School of Oriental and African Studies, University of London, and a Master's degree in Modern and Contemporary Chinese Literature from Fudan University in Shanghai. Fluent in Mandarin, Indre has lived in Beijing and Shanghai for more than ten years. Previously responsible for communications at a cross-border consultancy helping Western companies enter the Chinese market, she is now an independent researcher, writer, and translator. Indre lives in central Shanghai with her Shanghainese husband Ruiyu and son Roy.

KATHY FLOWER has worked in the UK and China as a BBC radio producer, TV presenter, scriptwriter, teacher, and trainer. She presented China's first major English-language teaching series, "Follow Me," on Chinese TV. She became known to hundreds of millions of enthusiastic Chinese viewers as "Fay-lau-ah *laoshi*," or "Teacher Flower." Back in London she joined BBC World Service Radio returning to China many times to work and to travel.

CONTENTS

MAP OF CHINA

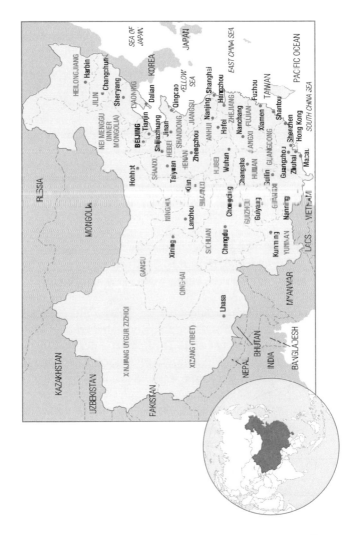

Since 1979, when Premier Deng Xiaoping declared China open for business, millions of its citizens have been lifted out of poverty and given the chance to control their own destinies. Initially China achieved its spectacular growth by "making and selling things we want at prices we can afford," as *The Economist* put it; four decades on, it is the world's second-largest economy, a major player on the global stage, courted by governments and multinationals worldwide, and ambitious to go even further.

Having become rich, new China has made peace with its past. Old China's once derelict temples and palaces have been restored to vibrant life and draw huge crowds, while new China's futuristic cities are on a par with Tokyo, London, or New York.

Behind these economic miracles lie the Chinese people, 1.4 billion individuals, each one part of a family unit. Where Western family sagas focus on illicit love affairs and property, Chinese family sagas offer a guide to the country's turbulent history. Perhaps most famous is Jung Chang's bestselling autobiography, *Wild Swans: Three Daughters of China*. The first daughter was Yu Fang, Jung Chang's grandmother; as a small child her feet were bound and then she was sold to a warlord as one of his concubines. Her daughter by him was to become Jung Chang's mother, Bao Qin, a founder member of China's Communist Party. Jung Chang, born in 1952, at first had a privileged childhood; but when the orchestrated chaos of Mao Zedong's Cultural Revolution began in the 1960s, her parents were denounced and tortured. Eventually Jung Chang gained a scholarship to England and left for good. Nowadays, generations of daughters (and sons) of China are free to study abroad, to travel, and to work toward their own dreams. But competition is fierce in today's market-oriented China, and traditional beliefs in the importance of hard work, a good education, and a supportive family are stronger than ever.

China's outward-looking economic agenda is very recent. In the past, its size meant it did not need to engage with anyone outside its borders. China saw itself as the center of the world; peoples on the periphery were considered barbarians, to be graciously received by the Emperor and then dismissed. From the sixteenth century onward, Europeans who tried to establish links with China were equally politely rebuffed.

After the Communist triumph in 1949, China remained closed to the West. Not until 1971 could US envoy Henry Kissinger go secretly to Beijing to meet Mao, followed in 1972 by President Nixon himself. But after Mao's death in 1976, Deng Xiaoping opened China's doors, putting it on the path to prosperity and changing it, and the world, in the process.

Nowadays, China is changing the world through its Belt and Road Initiative, a controversial infrastructure vision of mind-blowing proportions, active outbound mergers and acquisitions, and innovative technologies. There is incredible energy, ambition, and pace of change in this country that can easily leave one intoxicated. The Chinese you will meet in this fascinating country are well educated, warm, knowledgeable about world affairs, and keen to talk about everything under the sun. This book should help you to be a "good guest," whether you are there for work, pleasure, or both.

KEY FACTS

Official Name	The People's Republic of China (PRC); in Mandarin, *Zhonghua Renmin Gonghe Guo*	The island of Taiwan, which has its own government, calls itself the ROC (Republic of China).
Capital City	Beijing (Peking) *Bei* = north *jing* = capital	"Peking" is the old Wade–Giles form of transliterating the city's name.
Main Cities	Shanghai, Shenzhen, Guangzhou, Chongqing (Chunking), Chengdu, Tianjin, Harbin, Suzhou	Major ports include Shanghai, Hong Kong, Guangzhou (Canton), Qingdao (Tsingtao), Ningbo, Tianjin (Tientsin), and Qinhuangdao.
Area	3,695,500 sq. miles (9,571,300 sq. km)	The third-largest country in the world
Terrain	Mountains, deserts, and arid basins in the north and northwest. Mountainous in the south. Rolling hills and plains in the east.	Two-thirds mountain or desert. The low-lying east is irrigated by the rivers Huang He (Yellow River), Chang Jiang (Yangtze Kiang), and Xi Jiang (Si Kiang).
Climate	Temperatures vary greatly in the arid north and west, with hot summers and very cold dry winters.	The south and east are warm and humid, with rainfall all year-round.
Population	The world's most populous country: 1.4 billion	Roughly one in five people in the world live in China.
Population Density	Shanghai has 7,000 people per sq. mile; Beijing 1,927 per sq. mile; Tibet, only 5 people per sq. mile.	Most people live in the eastern central region, on the fertile flood plains and the eastern coastal region.

Urban/Rural Divide	The World Bank estimates that about 54% of China's population live and work in cities. Migrant workers from the countryside have powered the Chinese economy for four decades.	The household registration system (*hukou*) means that rural-born workers may live in cities for years, but still belong to their area of origin. They have been treated as second-class citizens, but are now claiming equality with city dwellers.
Ethnic Makeup	Roughly 92% are Han Chinese; the rest are made up of 55 officially recognized "national minorities."	Minorities are small in number but concentrated in border regions, thus politically important.
Age Structure	0–14 years: 17.2%; 15–64 years: 73.4%; 65 and over: 9.4%. China's one-child policy (1975–2015) has resulted in fewer young people than in most developing countries.	Healthcare has improved and the population is getting older: in 2020 11.8% of the population was over 65.
Life Expectancy	Men: 75; women: 78. The worldwide average is 70 for men, 74 for women.	Prior to 1949, historians say that average life expectancy was about 35 years.
Languages	Mandarin (official), Cantonese, Wu, and others. All share same script, though Taiwan and Hong Kong use traditional characters; the mainland uses simplified ones.	Other minority languages exist such as Tibetan, and more in the southwest, where the minorities mostly live.

Religion	Officially atheist. Traditionally Daoist, Confucian, and Buddhist. Minority religious groups: Muslim, Christian.	Christianity and Buddhism are growing in popularity. The Communist Party is cautiously tolerant of organized religion. Crackdowns are not uncommon.
Government	Ruled by the Communist Party since 1949. There are eight officially recognized other parties, but no general elections on the Western model.	These minority parties in reality have no power and are subservient to the CPC.
Economy	From 1979 China moved away from a Soviet-style centrally planned economy to a free market one, and now accounts for 17% of global economic activity.	Annual GDP growth of 10% since the 1990s slowed to 6% by 2019. Wages, however, continue to rise.
Currency	Renminbi, "people's currency." Also known as the yuan (dollar). 1 renminbi/yuan = 10 jiao = 100 fen	In transition from a "soft" to a "hard" currency. It is not yet freely convertible.
Resources	Natural resources such as gasoline, natural gas, coal, uranium; mineral resources incl. iron, manganese, and zinc; non-metallic mineral resources incl. graphite, phosphorus, and sulfur. China has the world's largest reserves of rare earth.	Deforestation in the southwest is being tackled by replanting. According to the UN FAO about 22% of China is covered by forest; about 5.6% of this is "primary forest", the most bio-diverse kind.

Agriculture	No longer self-sufficient in food, China imports food such as meat, soy, wheat, and dairy products.	Most milk is now imported from New Zealand. Food safety has become a major concern.
Main Exports	Electronic equipment, machines, engines, furniture, lighting, clothing, medical, plastics, vehicles.	China is the largest export economy in the world. It is also the second-largest importer in the world.
Electricity	220 volts, 50 Hz	Wall sockets have three connectors.
Media: Traditional	State-controlled and subject to censorship. *Renmin Ribao* (*People's Daily*) is the Party's main newspaper. Chinese Central TV (CCTV) is the state broadcaster.	There are about 3,000 regional TV and radio stations, and increasing numbers of foreign broadcasters.
Media: English Language	CCTV broadcasts in English and other foreign languages. There is an active (mostly state-run) English-language press.	*China Daily* is published six days a week, with a *Business Weekly* on Sunday.
Internet Domain	.cn The main search engine is Baidu.	The government monitors Internet use and employs "microblog monitors."
TV/DVD	PAL system used	
Telephone	International country code: 00 86	
Time Difference	GMT + 8 hrs	Although China extends across five time zones, Beijing time is used.

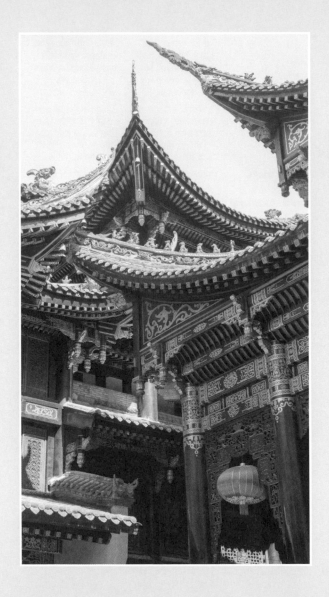

CHAPTER ONE

LAND & PEOPLE

"For millennia . . . Chinese civilization stretched over an area larger than any European state. Chinese language and culture . . . extended to every known terrain: steppes and pine forests in the north, shading into Siberia, tropical jungles and terraced rice farms in the south; from the coast with its canals, ports, and fishing villages, to the stark deserts of Central Asia and the ice capped peaks of the Himalayan frontier."

Henry Kissinger, *On China*, 2011.

TERRAIN AND CLIMATE

China has a total landmass of 3.7 million square miles (9.6 million sq. km), next in size only to Russia and Canada. At its maximum, it measures approximately 3,100 miles (5,000 km) north–south, and 3,230 miles (5,200 km) east–west. Its land border is 14,168 miles (22,800 km) long. Apart from the mainland, there are more than 5,400 islands, some just bare rocks that only

appear at low tide. Technically speaking, it encompasses five time zones from the east coast across to the Russian border in the west.

Most rivers flow west to east into the Pacific Ocean. The Yangtze River (Chang Jiang) is the longest at 3,915 miles (6,300 km)—and third longest in the world after the Nile and the Amazon—followed by the Yellow River (Huang He) at 3,395 miles (5,464 km), the birthplace of Chinese civilization. However, in recent years, the Yellow River has been shortened by several hundred miles for months on end, due to having dried up near its delta.

China is a land of extremes, and temperatures vary widely. In northern China, summers are hot and short, winters long and cold. The humidity in the north in summer is unpleasant—around 60–70 percent—and the lack of moisture in the winter, when humidity falls to about 2 percent, is even worse, as are the dust storms caused by sand blowing in from the Gobi Desert.

To the north of the capital, Beijing, lie the vast empty grasslands of the Inner Mongolian Plateau. Mongolia is swept by winds from Siberia and is bitterly cold in winter, sometimes as low as minus 35°C (-31°F), but with fine, sunny days. Harbin, China's northernmost major city, is famous for its annual winter display of huge sculptures made of ice blocks, taken from the Songhua River, and lit from inside by colored lanterns; starting around January 5, the festival lasts for about a month, until its sculptures start to melt away with the coming of spring. The south of China is more temperate, and in recent years northerners who can afford it have started retiring there to enjoy the milder climate—the tropical island of Hainan in particular is popular. In the south, vegetation remains green all year-round. The coastal regions are warm and humid, with four distinct seasons. The south and southwest of China have a much more agreeable climate, with lush green vegetation and beautiful wooded mountains wreathed in mists. The southwest is the home of bamboo forests and the panda; also of many plants familiar in the West, such as rhododendrons, some of which were brought over to Europe by nineteenth-century botanists.

China is a country of superlatives. The world's highest mountain, Mount Everest (Zhumulangma Feng in Chinese), forms China's western border with Nepal and India. It is part of the Himalayan range of mountains, forty of whose peaks rise to over 22,900 feet (7,000 m). In the northwest is the Tarim Basin, the largest inland

Wulong National Park in Chongqing, southwest China.

basin in the world. To the east of the Tarim Basin is the low-lying Turpan depression, called the "Oasis of Fire," the hottest place in China, with temperatures of up to 120°F (49°C) in summer. Xinjiang, home to Uyghurs, an ethnic minority of Turkic people, is also home to the Taklamakan, the largest desert in China. The oasis towns of the vast empty desert areas were used for two thousand years as stopovers on the Silk Route—from the time of the Romans, caravans of camels would carry silk to the West. Salt from China's largest salt lake, Lop Nur, also went this way. Whoever controlled the

The Li River in Guilin, southeast China.

oases could tax this traffic, so despite its arid deserts, Xinjiang was an attractive prize. Today, it remains so for its vast reserves of oil and gas.

Only about 20 percent of the terrain is suitable for agriculture. The majority of the Han population has for centuries lived mainly on the fertile floodplains at the lower reaches of the Yellow River and the Yangtze River. These two rivers deposit silt, which makes the flood plain the richest agricultural area in China. This is where the main cities have grown up, along with key industries. So much of China is uninhabitable that

19

around 90 percent of the people, mainly Han Chinese, are squeezed into about half of the area. The government has tried to resettle people in more sparsely populated areas, such as Tibet and Xinjiang, but the Han do not really want to live there and the locals are not keen to have them.

Nowadays China's ambitions are much more futuristic: the government is trying to spur urbanization by creating new cities and districts and encouraging the rural population living in the vicinity to move in; there are nearly 600 more cities now than when the Communists took over in 1949. Some have become jaw-dropping successes, such as Shanghai's futuristic Pudong district. Once mocked by foreign analysts as a "ghost town," it now boasts the highest GDP of all

Shanghai districts, and has become the backdrop of many a Hollywood movie. Or take Shenzhen: in a matter of thirty-something years it has grown from a humble market town to an ultra-modern megacity, whose economy has already surpassed that of neighboring Hong Kong. Not all new Chinese cities have been as successful, however. So-called ghost towns do exist. Building a new city can be a relatively quick process, but putting in place the necessary infrastructure, jobs and services for anything up to a few million people inevitably takes time. But the Chinese traditionally take a long-term view of things, and these new cities, for all their eerie emptiness, are part of that vision: to the government, the question is not whether they will fill up, but when.

HAN CHINESE AND MINORITY NATIONALITIES

Ninety-two percent of the population of China are of the Han race, or what the West is accustomed to call Chinese. Minority nationalities generally live in the northwestern and southwestern extremities of the country. Often, people belonging to ethnic minorities outwardly don't look any different from the Han, especially to the Western eye; others, such as Uyghurs or Huis, stand out quite a bit. Fifty-five minority nationalities are officially recognized, totalling just over 100 million people. They have their own customs, languages, dress, and religions. Many in the northwest, near the borders with Pakistan, Afghanistan, India, and Russia, are Muslim, most notably the Huis and Uyghurs. Tibetans, Mongolians, Tus, Lhobas, and Monbas largely follow Tibetan Buddhism. The Dai, Blang, and De'ang people profess another ancient branch of Buddhism, while many others follow animism, folk religions, and ancestor worship.

Mandarin is the only the official language and all minority peoples learn it, although many beyond a certain age may still be unable to speak any Mandarin at all. The government has helped to create written languages for ten minority nationalities, including the Zhuang, Bouyei, Miao, Dong, Hani, and Li, which prior to 1949 had only spoken languages. The minority nationalities have a geopolitical importance far beyond their numbers because of the strategic territories they occupy along China's sparsely populated and porous frontiers; it was partly because of this that they were exempted from the government's One-Child Policy (see page 39). Official attitudes toward them are a complex mixture of tolerance and control. People belonging to ethnic minorities largely keep to themselves and remain somewhat isolated from the Han. The government has put policies in place in an attempt to better integrate them into mainstream society and the economy—a more positive example of which would be the preferential treatment people from minority communities receive when applying for college. However, many minority peoples remain marginalized. Integration policies have been more aggressive in northwestern regions.

A BRIEF HISTORY

The fertile floodplains of the Yellow River were the cradle of Chinese civilization. Thousands of years ago the Chinese were already weaving silk, carving jade, casting bronze, growing wheat, millet, and rice, and recording events in a written language. The crossbow, used in Europe in the Middle Ages, was invented in China some fifteen centuries earlier. A thousand years before the Industrial Revolution in Britain, China already had coke ovens and steel blast furnaces. Chinese art, science, architecture, language, literature, and philosophy continue to be studied and admired around the world.

The Chinese will tell you, with pride, of their five thousand years of civilization, but in fact it goes back even further. Archaeologists have found evidence of Neolithic sites dating from before 5000 BCE. The earliest-known dynasty was the Xia, which ruled about 1994–1523 BCE. By the time of the Shang (or Yin) dynasty, which flourished in the Yellow River valley in 1523–1027 BCE, a sophisticated culture had developed, with advanced bronze-manufacturing, a written language, and the first Chinese calendar.

The Zhou and the Mandate of Heaven
The last Shang ruler was a tyrant who was overthrown by the founders of the Zhou dynasty (1027–255 BCE). This period saw the introduction of money, iron, written laws, and the ethical philosophy of Confucianism, and gave birth to the idea of the "Mandate of Heaven" (*Tianming*), in which Heaven gives wise rulers a mandate to rule, but

takes it away from unworthy ones. The Emperor became known as the "Son of Heaven," a concept that still had potency right up until Mao Zedong's death in 1976. Later, the "Mandate of Heaven" incorporated the Daoist belief that Heaven sends natural disasters such as earthquakes and floods to show its disapproval of bad rulers.

During the Zhou period the Chinese people's sense of their unique identity and cultural superiority developed. The name *Zhongguo*, or "Middle Kingdom," was coined to describe the central importance of China: anyone outside it was considered to be a barbarian. *Zhongguo* is still the name used by the Chinese today to refer to China; foreigners are referred to as *waiguoren*, or "outside country people."

The Warring States Period (c. 500–221 BCE)

Civil war followed the Zhou dynasty's reign, and the Zhou empire broke up into small kingdoms. The philosopher Confucius declared that the Zhou empire had been a golden age, and for centuries afterward the Chinese looked back on it as an ideal time. Eventually, the Qin (pronounced "Chin") dynasty defeated its rivals and united the warring feudal states into a single empire.

The Qin Dynasty (221–207 BCE)

The Qin introduced centralized government, standard weights and measures, writing systems, and money, and built a network of roads that joined the capital (near modern-day Xi'an) to the distant outposts of the empire. The first Qin Emperor, Qin Shi Huang, used thousands of slaves to continue the building of the Great Wall of China, designed

to keep out the "Mongol hordes." Much of the original Great Wall has collapsed, its stones carted off to build houses for the locals—whose ancestors helped to build the original wall. Most of the parts that are still standing have been heavily restored and are visited by millions every year.

Qin Shi Huang was buried in Chang'an (today Xi'an). With him were buried the now world-famous terracotta army of around 8,000 life size-soldiers, 130 chariots, and 670 horses, who stand guard over him; using clay figures brought to an end the barbaric tradition of burying real people alive to escort the Emperor's body into the next world.

The Han Dynasty (206 BCE–9 CE and 25–220 CE)
The Han dynasty saw the Chinese empire expand into central Asia, and the growth of centralized rule. The position of the Emperor changed from that of sole and absolute ruler to one in which power was delegated to a highly developed civil service. A notoriously complicated and rigid examination system, based on the candidates'

knowledge of classic Confucian texts, was set up to select people to work as bureaucrats; it lasted more or less unchanged for two thousand years. Ever since, the Chinese people have referred to themselves as the *Han; Hanyu* is the Chinese language, and *Hanzi* is the name for Chinese characters.

The Sui Dynasty (581–618)
External rebellions and internal feuding eventually destroyed the Han and the empire split into three competing kingdoms, resulting in the eventual victory of the Wei over the Chou and Wu. Confucianism was superseded by Buddhism, introduced from India, and by Daoism; and "barbarian" (known in the West as the Hun) invasions started in the north. The Sui dynasty then reunified China, halted the march of the Huns, and strengthened the Great Wall.

The Tang Dynasty (618–906)
The Sui were soon replaced by the Tang. This was a golden age for China. The Tang capital was in modern day Xi'an. Then called Chang'an, it was one of the world's greatest cities, rivaling Rome and Constantinople, with a population of one million and a society with many modern features such as commerce, tax collection, civil administration, tolerance of different religions, and a thriving culture. The Tang era is famous for its poetry and ceramics. The Tang continued the creation of canals linking different parts of the empire, and built inns for traveling officials, merchants, and pilgrims to break their journeys. There was more contact with foreigners than at

any other time until the late twentieth century. The Tang empire disintegrated into the "Five Dynasties and Ten Kingdoms," amid war and economic decline.

The Song Dynasty (960–1279)

Under the Song, China was unified again, and order restored. This was a period of calm and creativity. However, the frontiers were neglected, and Mongol incursions began. Despite the Middle Kingdom's attempts to seal itself off from the outside world, foreigners continued to find their way in, as invaders, ambassadors, or merchants. The most famous traveler of all, Venetian merchant and explorer Marco Polo, visited China from 1275 to 1292. On his return to Venice he wrote the first eyewitness account of China, describing its wealthy cities, paper money, methods of salt production, and the burning of coal to create heat. His book inspired others such as Christopher Columbus to want to travel to China and a version of it has been in print ever since.

Some Chinese "Firsts"

The Chinese are proud of their "Four Great Inventions": papermaking, the compass, gunpowder, and printing. Engraved woodblock printing on paper and silk was invented in the seventh century; the world's oldest surviving printed book is a Chinese Buddhist text printed in 868 CE. Another Chinese first was the invention of moveable type in the eleventh century.

The Yuan Dynasty (1260–1368)

By the time of Marco Polo's arrival in China, the Mongols had poured across the Gobi Desert on their horses, undeterred by the Great Wall. They made Beijing their capital and Kublai Khan became the first emperor of the foreign Yuan dynasty— the first non-native emperor to conquer all of China. The Yuan were ruthless but efficient rulers; they improved the roads leading into China and Russia, promoted trade, and even set up a famine relief system.

The Ming Dynasty (1368–1644)

The Yuan were driven out, to be replaced by the first emperor of the native Han Chinese Ming dynasty, Zhu Yuanzhang, a man of poor peasant stock. Famine, natural disasters, hyperinflation, and corruption brought Ming rule to an end, hastened by an earthquake in 1556 that is thought to have killed 830,000 people. This sign that the emperor had lost the Mandate of Heaven strengthened his enemies; echoes of this belief were heard when the Tangshan earthquake of July 1976 killed about 240,000 people, just three months before Mao died.

The First Europeans Arrive

In 1516, two hundred and forty-one years after Marco
Polo, Portuguese ships arrived off the coast of China.
Portugal in the sixteenth century was a great trading
nation with imperial ambitions, and the Portuguese
were allowed to set up a trading post in Macau, to be
followed by the British, Dutch, and Spanish. In 1582
an Italian Jesuit priest named Matteo Ricci arrived in
Macau, learned Chinese, and then settled in Zhaoqing at
the invitation of the governor, who had heard of Ricci's
knowledge of mathematics and cartography. Ricci made
the first European-style world map in Chinese; he also
compiled a Portuguese–Chinese dictionary. Six copies of
the original map on rice paper, made in 1602, still survive
and there is a plaque commemorating Ricci in Zhaoqing.

The Qing Dynasty (1644–1912)

The Ming were succeeded by another non-Chinese
dynasty, the Qing, nomads from Manchuria who, like all
the other foreign rulers, soon assimilated into Chinese
culture. The Qing government kept the Europeans as
far away as possible, making them stay in Canton (now
Guangzhou). But this did not prevent the start of a trade
that was to become a byword for Western imperialism:
the sale by the British of Indian-grown opium to the
Chinese.

Opium had been used for centuries for pain relief,
as an antidepressant, and to kill hunger pains. People
were well aware of the risk of addiction, but nonetheless
opium remained legal in Europe and the USA as late as
the 1920s.

The Opium Wars

In exchange for selling opium the British were at last getting all the Chinese tea, silk, and porcelain they craved. But the numbers of addicts were growing rapidly, and the Chinese Emperor tried to ban the trade in 1800; his decree was ignored. The trade continued unchecked until 1839, when the Chinese seized and burned 20,000 chests of opium. So began the first of the notorious Opium Wars (1839–42), with the British attacking Canton, forcing China to cede Hong Kong and to open five ports to European trade. The Second Opium War (1856-60), fought by the British with support from the Russians, French, and Americans, was just as notorious and understandably influenced the Chinese view of Westerners as "foreign devils" for the next hundred years: one of the worst episodes was the looting and burning of the two Summer Palaces, seasonal residences of the imperial family, by the joint Western forces.

By 1860 the West had won huge concessions: foreigners could settle in many different parts of China, were exempt from Chinese laws, and the Chinese were forced to pay large war indemnities. The Chinese, on the other hand, felt beyond humiliated; national morale hit an all-time low in 1895 when China was defeated by Japan in the First Sino-Japanese war. Previously seen as little more than a cultural disciple and a vassal state, Japan ended up surpassing its master—it managed to become a modern industrial nation long before China did.

As the nineteenth century drew to a close, the Throne of Heaven was occupied by the four-year-old Emperor, Guangxu, but real power lay in the hands of his aunt,

大清國慈禧皇太后

An oil painting of Dowager Empress Cixi by Dutch artist Huber Vos in 1905.

the Dowager Empress Cixi. Forward-thinking Chinese intellectuals pleaded with the court to implement reforms to modernize the country but were met with either hostility or indifference. While Western powers and the Japanese were growing in strength thanks to evolving technologies, China was regressing and only growing weaker.

The Boxer Rebellion

Worse was to come. The Dowager Empress raised taxes and added to the misery of the peasantry. War, floods, famine, and drought plagued the last years of the dying century, with the foreign powers profiting at China's expense. Peasant anger erupted in the Boxer Rebellion.

The anti-Western Society of the Harmonious Fist, known as the "Boxers," was born in Shangdong province and nurtured by the weakened Qing government, who saw their popularity with the peasantry as a chance to chase foreigners out of China. The Boxers massacred foreign missionaries and Chinese Christians, destroyed churches and railway lines, and, in 1900, marched to Beijing and attacked the foreign compounds.

Rapid intervention by foreign troops meant that the Boxers lost, but secret societies aimed at toppling the Qing dynasty and getting rid of the foreigners were springing up all over China. In 1905 Dr. Sun Yat-sen, still revered today as the father of modern China, became the leader of one of these revolutionary groups, the Guomindang (National People's Party), and events started to move fast. The Dowager Empress died in 1908, as did Guangxu, and the two-year-old Pu Yi came to the throne—later immortalized in Bertolucci's memorable film *The Last Emperor* (1987). The little boy's reign was brief. In 1911, the Xinhai Revolution, led by Sun Yat-sen, rolled across China. The Qing government acknowledged defeat, Pu Yi was made to abdicate, and in 1912 Sun Yat-sen proclaimed the Republic of China.

Warlords, Nationalists, and Communists

After the abdication of the infant emperor, Yuan Shikai, a key figure in the Qing military and politics, managed to attain the position of first President of the Republic of China in exchange for support of the revolutionaries; however, he soon fell into autocratic ways. On his death in 1916, central government collapsed and warlords ruled over small local fiefdoms. Extreme poverty and lawlessness were rife. In 1921 Dr. Sun Yat-sen was elected President of the nominal National Government; the same year saw the founding of the Chinese Communist Party, which had strong links with the new Soviet regime in neighboring Russia. From 1923 the Communists worked with the Guomindang to reunite China and gradually won the support of the Chinese peasants. But when Sun Yat-sen died in 1925, the new leader of the Guomindang, Chiang Kai-shek, declared war on the Communists.

Civil war began in 1926 and living conditions for the poor, already bad, deteriorated even further. American journalist Edgar Snow and other contemporary writers described in shocking detail how children worked in factories for twelve hours a day, hundreds starved to death on the streets, and how every night carts trundled through the cities, gathering up corpses as though they were so much rubbish. While the Communists and the Guomindang were fighting each other for control of China, the Japanese overran Manchuria in 1932, and set up the puppet state of Manchukuo. In 1937 they attacked Shanghai. During the Second World War the various political groups united against the Japanese invaders, but from 1941 Chiang Kai-shek received help from the USA and Britain, which was to poison relations with Mao for many years afterward. For many older Chinese, Japanese brutality during the war has not been forgotten.

The Long March
In 1934–5 the Communists undertook the "Long March" from southeast to northwest China to escape encirclement by the Guomindang. Open civil war resumed in 1946,

and in 1949 the Red Army led by Mao Zedong defeated the Nationalists at Nanjing. Chiang Kai-shek fled to the island of Formosa (now Taiwan), taking with him the entire gold reserves of his impoverished country. On October 1, 1949—now National Day and a public holiday—Mao

Zedong, standing atop the Gate of Heavenly Peace, facing a 250,000 strong crowd in Tiananmen Square, declared the People's Republic of China.

The People's Republic
For a while daily life improved for most Chinese, and some look back on the early 1950s as the best period of Mao's rule. But in 1958 the "Great Leap Forward," the ideologically driven five-year plan to accelerate the economy, marked the beginning of campaigns driven by blind ideology rather than pragmatism. Impractical policies, coupled with flooding and drought in 1959 and 1960, led to famine; after the Sino–Soviet split in 1960, the Soviet Union stopped giving aid to China. In the mid-1960s, Deng Xiaoping (who later became president) and Liu Shaoqi held considerable power. Free markets were encouraged, peasants were allowed to own land, and the Soviet-influenced policies that had failed so disastrously were, all too briefly, abandoned.

The Cultural Revolution (1966–76)
Mao felt that China was slipping back into its capitalist ways, and in May 1966 he unleashed the "Great Proletarian Cultural Revolution," whose shock troops were teenage Red Guards. Its aim was "to hold aloft the banner of Mao Zedong's thought . . . struggle against the capitalist roaders . . . transform education, literature, and art . . . and facilitate the development of the socialist system." For ten years, until Mao's death in 1976, China was engulfed in cruelty and orchestrated chaos. Schools and universities were closed, millions of urban youths,

some barely out of primary school, were forced to leave their homes and move to remote rural areas to do manual labor; teachers were humiliated and persecuted; anyone labeled an intellectual or capitalist could be tortured, killed, or sent to labor in atrocious conditions. Red Guards parading their victims around so onlookers could beat them, spit at them and insult them became a daily sight, as did dead bodies lying in the streets. It is one of the darkest chapters in the history of contemporary China; distrust and paranoia were pervasive, as friends turned against friends, and neighbors against neighbors—as little as a single phrase could end your life as you knew it. Millions died, many committing suicide in despair. It is almost impossible to reconcile this decade of collective madness and brutality with today's vibrant, confident China—but it happened.

The Open Door Policy

Mao belatedly supported the efforts of Prime Minister Zhou Enlai to restore order in 1970. A window of opportunity to stop the chaos opened in 1972 with President Nixon's visit to China. Eventually, one year after Mao's death and the arrest of his wife Jiang Qing and the other members of the infamous "Gang of Four," blamed for the disasters of the Cultural Revolution, Deng Xiaoping, supreme survivor against the odds, returned to power.

Deng's greatest achievement was setting Chinese economic reform in motion. His model, termed "Socialism with Chinese characteristics," saw China rejoin the global community on which it had for so long turned its back. More importantly, it lifted millions of

Chinese out of poverty and laid the groundwork for China to become the economic powerhouse that it is today. Deng was a pragmatist: his famous statement that "It does not matter what color the cat is, so long as it catches mice," was the antithesis of Mao's dogmatism. He transformed China into a market economy, encouraged

entrepreneurship, foreign trade and investment, and his successors have continued to develop these policies.

Since 1979, China's economy has doubled roughly every seven-and-a-half years. Frenetic economic growth has served to transform all spheres of public and private life, including education, entertainment, and culture, not to mention the collective mindset. Deng Xiaoping's famous utterance "To get rich is glorious," a far cry from Mao's "The poorer the better," has been widely internalized and universally embraced.

Turn of the Millennium

The end of the twentieth century saw a number of milestones, among them the pro-democracy protests in Tiananmen Square in 1989. The government's response to the peaceful protests crushed the hopes many intellectuals and students had nurtured throughout the '80s, that economic development would eventually translate into political reform. Though shocking, the events did not plunge China back into the turmoil many had feared; both the government and the general population chose to prioritize stability and continued economic development instead.

Other milestones included the unexpectedly peaceful handover of the British-leased territory of Hong Kong and the Portuguese-governed enclave of Macau back to Chinese rule in 1997 and 1999 respectively. The twenty-first century has produced more milestones: China's entry into the World Trade Organization in 2001, after fifteen years of negotiations, and Beijing's hosting of the Olympics in 2008.

China Today

China's ambitions have long outgrown its national borders. Many of them are embedded in the ongoing Belt and Road Initiative (also known as "One Belt, One Road"), which has caused a great deal of controversy since it was first announced by President Xi Jinping in 2013. The loosely defined multiproject initiative aims to build infrastructure connecting Asian, European, and African countries with China in what has been dubbed the "New Silk Road." Outside China, it has raised a lot of concerns about the Middle Kingdom's economic imperialism. There is, however, no denying its jaw-dropping scope: China's planned investment in the project amounts to US $1 trillion. As part of the Belt and Road Initiative, for instance, China has set up (with an initial capital of US $100 billion) and is financing the Asian Infrastructure Investment Bank (AIIB), to support construction in other parts of Asia. It will doubtless rival the IMF and the World Bank, seen by some in Asia as dominated by Western countries.

Though India is fast catching up, for now China remains the most populous country in the world. For thirty years after the founding of the PRC in 1949, couples were encouraged to produce ever more infant revolutionaries and the population doubled. "The more Chinese, the better," said Mao; so the traditional Chinese desire for big families went unchecked until the adoption of the one-child family policy in 1979. The government tried by every possible means to enforce this unpopular measure.

"Fewer births, better births," 1987.

By official estimates, it resulted in "only" 25 million babies being born each year. But the Chinese are living to a ripe old age, so there is a lack of young workers to pay for the increasing numbers of senior citizens.

In October 2015, the end of the one-child policy was announced, and all families are now allowed, indeed encouraged, to have two children. The baby boom the government had hoped would materialize, however, so far has not. According to a 2019 study released by the Chinese Academy of Social Sciences, the country will enter an "era of negative population growth" by 2030, though other studies predict the population will already begin to fall by 2024. The study warned that, unless there is a drastic change in trends, the population figures by 2065 will resemble those last seen in the mid-1990s: this does not bode well for the world's second-largest economy. See Chapter 5 for more on this topic.

New Urban Citizens

Today, close to 60 percent of the population live in cities, and rates of urbanization show no sign of slowing down. To ease the pressure on its swelling megacities, the government is building much-needed new ones. China now has more than a hundred cities with a population of over one million; the US has ten. Beijing, Shanghai, and Chongqing are three of the most densely populated, with Shanghai clocking up a tremendous 7,000 people per square mile (2,700 per sq. km).

GOVERNMENT AND THE ECONOMY

Rich and Poor

According to the World Bank, some 850 million Chinese have been lifted out of poverty since 1978, the year Deng

Xiaoping kickstarted economic reforms. However, income disparities have increased. The growing income inequality is seen most clearly in the differences in living standards between the urban, coastal areas and the rural, inland regions. While there still are some forty-five million people—roughly 3 percent of the population—living below the poverty line (defined by the government as surviving on less than US $1 a day) and hundreds of millions subsisting barely above it, a new billionaire is made every two to three days. In fact, Beijing is now the ultimate billionaire city: there are more billionaires who call the Chinese capital home than any other city worldwide.

There have also been increases in the inequality of the provision of healthcare and education, partly due to growing costs (in most cases, quality healthcare and education are only free on paper), and partly due to the rigid Household Registration system (*hukou*), which stipulates that residents can only get access to education, healthcare and other services where they are registered as living. The outdated system has given rise to a series of social issues, such as the phenomenon of "left-behind children," whereby rural migrant workers are forced to leave their children behind in their villages because they would be ineligible for schools in the cities they work in. In this situation it is not unusual for parents and children to be together only once a year, typically during the New Year holidays. There has been some talk of the *hukou* system being done away with in the near future, but for the moment it is going strong. Growing discontent with social and income inequality amid slowing economic growth is seen as the greatest risk to China's internal stability.

On the whole, however, the overall increase in prosperity is undeniable. While critics express skepticism, the government seems on track with its goal to eradicate absolute poverty; it reports that some 13 million people were lifted out of poverty in 2017 alone. Only time will tell if the change is sustainable.

THE POLITICAL LANDSCAPE

The Communist Party of China was founded on July 23, 1921 and has ruled China since October 1, 1949. In mid-2018, it was reported to have some 87.8 million members, or 6.28 percent of the population. Membership of the Communist Party is no longer the prerequisite for getting a job, housing, or education that it once was, however. In fact, joining the Party has become rather a lengthy and complicated process that can take up to a year or more. As the Party attempts to build something of a meritocracy, professing ideological allegiance is no longer enough—one must also prove a level of academic attainment, technical aptitude, and certain moral qualities. The Party is still not democratically accountable and China's economic progress has not been matched by political change. Stability and continued economic growth are prized above all else.

Current President Xi Jinping is seen as China's most powerful political figure since Mao. Very different from his predecessors, who were seen as little more than efficient meritocrats working as a team, Xi has managed to centralize unprecedented power in his hands since taking the reigns in 2012. Constitutional amendments that removed the two-term presidential limit in 2018 mean Xi can now remain in office for life. Popular with the masses for his anti-corruption campaign, efforts to alleviate poverty, and more assertive foreign policy, Xi has managed to tighten government control on every aspect of public life in China. While it is not something that may be immediately obvious to a visitor—life in China's cities seems nothing short of vibrant, spirited, and diverse—there has been a definite change in the atmosphere. While in private some might not shy away from sharing their frank opinions on politics and society, a large part of the population, particularly those under the age of thirty-five, declare themselves completely apolitical; they simply don't feel that politics has anything to do with them.

Despite the government's popular efforts against corruption, there are still incidences of malpractice, including suppression of workers' protests and rights violations, many of which go unreported by the government-controlled media. People often still feel that their only recourse to justice is to take to the streets. Though public protests have generally reduced in size, official Chinese figures record hundreds of them every year.

China heavily monitors the Internet and blocks sites it deems harmful to national (or Party) interests. The system is referred to as "The Great Firewall of China." Google, as well as most Western social media Web sites such as Facebook, YouTube, WhatsApp, Twitter, Instagram, Reddit, Pinterest, and Quora have been banned; neither can one access Web sites of some of the key names in Western media, including *The New York Times*, Bloomberg, *The Independent*, BBC, *Wall Street Journal*, *The Economist*, *Time*, and others. Search terms such as Falun Gong (a banned religious group) are blocked. Savvy Internet users have been known to keep one step ahead and gain anonymous access to banned Web sites via VPN (virtual private network) technology. The government runs periodical crackdowns on VPN software. It is not recommended to discuss its use on Chinese social media, and particularly vigorous activity on, say, Twitter may earn you a visit from the Public Security Bureau. That being said, both expats and locals still manage to do plenty of googling and posting on Instagram. Cell phone video footage of incidents, such as of the huge explosion at the chemical plant in Tianjin in the summer of 2015, can often go viral on social media before official censorship is able to stop its circulation.

GREATER CHINA

The term encompasses mainland China as well as Hong Kong, Macau, and Taiwan, and is primarily used to designate cultural and economic, and, to a lesser extent, political ties. Hong Kong, a colony of the British Empire since the Opium Wars of the mid-nineteenth century, was handed back to the PRC in 1997; Macau, controlled by the Portuguese for centuries, was returned in 1999. Taiwan, an island 110 miles (180 km) away from southeastern coast of the mainland, has been known as the Republic of China (ROC) since the Guomindang disembarked on its shores following its defeat in the civil war in 1949. Taiwan remains a sensitive topic: many mainlanders feel it is only a question of time until it will be reintegrated into the rest of the country.

Hong Kong

One of the two special administrative regions (SAR) of China along with Macau, Hong Kong has the highest degree of autonomy in China's administrative system. The city was promised that under the "One China, Two Systems" principle no major changes would take place before 2047; however, political control here too has been tightening. There is still a (relatively) free press, though it treads lightly.

Widespread protests that began in 2019 cast the territory's political future into uncertainty. For many, the controversial Hong Kong national security law, enacted by the leadership in Beijing in June 2020, was the beginning of the end of the "One China, Two Systems" framework. There are fears that the law, which defines four broad offences (secession, subversion, terrorism, and collusion) as endangering national security with foreign forces, will allow Beijing to silence dissident voices in the city once and for all.

Hong Kong has retained many features of traditional Chinese culture that were banned for years in the PRC, along with the vibrancy and the strong work ethic that made it so successful economically. During its heyday in the 1980s and '90s, Hong Kong's popular movies and music shaped a whole generation of Chinese; the city was something of a dream destination. In recent years, however, its economy has become increasingly stagnant, while that of the mainland continues to grow. In fact, neighboring Shenzhen's economy overtook that of Hong Kong in 2018.

Macau

Macau, a tiny strip of the mainland's southern peninsula and a couple of islands west of Hong Kong, is home to only 650,000 people. Don't be fooled by the seemingly inconsequential figure—it is the most densely populated place on earth. It also has one of the world's highest life expectancy rates. The Portuguese practiced a relaxed form of colonialism in Macau, which included legalizing gambling in the mid-nineteenth century. Macau remains the only place in Greater China where gambling is legal, and so it is perhaps no wonder that the size of its gambling industry is six or seven times that of Las Vegas. From the mainland and Hong Kong people arrive daily by the busload (or designer sports car) to visit Macau's many casinos. It is here that the fantastically rich and mere mortals with a little money to spare rub shoulders and let their hair down. It is a fascinating place in the daytime too, where charming faded colonial relics contrast with brash new developments.

Taiwan

Some 2 million people, comprising the political elites, military personnel, and supporters of the Guomindang, fled to Taiwan in 1949; it became the rump of what had been known as the Republic of China. Technically, the PRC and the ROC remain at war, as no agreement ending it was ever signed. Taiwan has its own democratically elected government, but only a handful of countries officially recognize it as a nation state and it does not have a seat at the UN. Both the PRC government and mainlanders view it as a province of China that will sooner or later come back under its authority. Although there is significant and growing economic activity between China and Taiwan, political tensions have escalated anew in recent years.

THE ENVIRONMENT

Pollution

Respiratory and heart disease related to air pollution are a major cause of death in China. According to a 2018 study by the Chinese University of Hong Kong, it accounts for as many as 1.1 million premature deaths per year. Much energy production is still dependent on coal, and the resultant air pollution is particularly bad in northern regions during the winter months. Some cities can be shrouded in haze for days on end. While there is a lot of discontent regarding pollution, residents have done what they can to adapt: people check air quality apps before letting their children out to play, there is every kind of pollution-filtering face mask available on the market, and those who can afford it equip their home with air purifiers. It has become popular for businesses, from private kindergartens to ride-hailing apps, to offer a filtered air environment in order to attract potential customers.

China's economic development has taken its toll on the environment in other ways too. Waste from factories and sewers is poured into China's rivers and lakes; much of the water is anaerobic, that is, devoid of oxygen and supporting no life at all, apart from algae. It is reckoned that the area of desert increases every year by about 950 square miles (2,460 sq. km).

The government is only too aware of the problem, and in recent years has sought to find a delicate balance between fighting pollution without sacrificing economic growth. At the Climate Change Conference in Paris in 2015, China joined 195 signatories committed to cutting emissions to reduce global warming. In September 2016, on the eve of the G20 leaders' summit in Hangzhou—the first to be held in China—Presidents Xi Jinping and Barack Obama jointly announced the ratification of the Paris Agreement.

A number of innovative strategies have emerged as a result. In Beijing, for example, you can only drive your car on alternate days, depending on whether the last digit on your license plate is odd or even. In Shanghai, an annual quota of license plates issued means they could cost more than the car itself—unless, that is, you buy an electric vehicle, in which case it is free. Broad public awareness of environmental protection, however, is still very much in its infancy, and new urban consumption habits, such as online shopping sprees and cheap 24-hour food delivery, only further contribute to the problem.

China has big plans for renewable energy. As it moves away from coal toward greener energy solutions, it has become the world's largest manufacturer and consumer of solar panels. China's investment in and use of wind, hydro, and nuclear power sources is growing too.

COVID-19 IN CHINA

In early 2020, just before Chinese New Year, the capital of Hubei province, Wuhan, became the first epicenter of a baffling new disease. From this major logistic and university hub, it radiated out across China and the world. Such was the beginning of the global Covid-19 pandemic.

One day before New Year's Eve, Wuhan and the rest of Hubei were put under lockdown. But millions had already left—not to flee the disease, but rather to travel home for the holidays, and so most of the country soon found itself under similar, albeit milder, measures.

The Chinese mostly accepted these measures with stoic compliance. The general line of thinking was that China was sacrificing one province to save the rest of the country and indeed the world, and that everyone should put up with the temporary inconveniences.

A rare instance of mass anger toward the authorities ignited China's social media when Li Wenliang, one of the doctors who first discussed the dangers of transmission and who was subsequently reprimanded, died of the virus. In an equally rare move, the authorities investigated the matter immediately and apologized to Dr. Li's family.

Whereas the pandemic tarnished the CPC's image globally, at home the Party's resolute—if heavy-handed—tackling of the outbreak earned the population's forgiveness for its early mismanagement, and indeed consolidated the Party's position. People felt that the government managed to rectify its initial faults, showed respect for human life and chose its citizens' safety over economic loss.

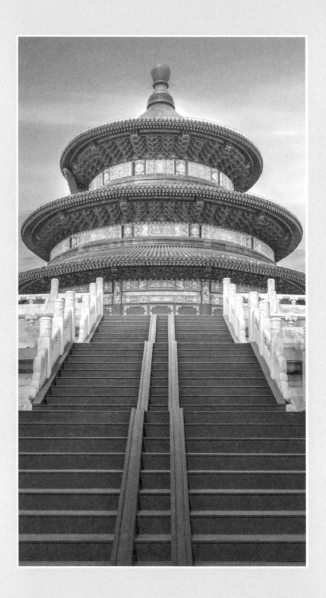

CHAPTER TWO

VALUES &
ATTITUDES

SCHOOLS OF THOUGHT

The history of China has been built on social order and the avoidance of chaos, or *luan*. The four major cultural factors that have influenced the development of its society in the past three millennia are the philosophies of Confucianism, Legalism, Daoism, and Maoism/Marxism.

Confucianism

The ethical system first laid down by Confucius in the sixth century BCE emphasized virtue, promotion of merit by scholarship, devotion to the family, and justice. The essentially conservative tenets of the sage have in recent years been invoked by the Communist Party in the interests of creating a more united, but also a more conformist, nation. For some, Confucianism is credited with helping China survive numerous difficulties, and its teachings are seen as compatible with the need for courtesy, justice, and honor. Others consider Confucianism as a bulwark of feudalism and sexism.

A key Confucianist value that is evident in daily life is filial piety: reverence and respect for one's elders and ancestors.

Legalism
The Legalists had their moment of glory at the time of Emperor Qin Shi Huang's reunification of the divided land in 221 BCE. To the Legalists, man was born sinful, and only the full force of law ruthlessly applied could quell his baser impulses. Some commentators see the centralized power of the state in China today as inspired by Legalism.

Daoism
The joyful, irreverent, quietist philosophy of Daoism, enunciated by the sage Laozi (born about 570 BCE),

A Daoist temple.

rejected both the moral idealism of Confucianism and the laws of Legalism as products of social contrivance. For Daoists, justice flowed from living in a state of harmony with the natural world.

Marxism and Maoism

The writings of Karl Marx, which had such an influence on the nineteenth- and twentieth-century revolutionaries, were rooted in the rationalism of the Enlightenment and the morality of the Judeo–Christian religious tradition. Dr. Sun Yat-sen and many early Chinese revolutionaries were equally influenced by Christian ideas of good and evil. Basic concepts of social equality and sharing wealth were fundamental to these early revolutionaries.

"Be a New Type of Worker, Lettered and Militarized," 1965.

The Chinese Communist Party borrowed many ideas from its Soviet counterpart, and it was not until 1949 that Mao Zedong's thought developed independently. Mao constantly urged the Chinese to identify with the peasants and with the poorer members of society, so the slogan "the poorer the better" became part of China's thinking in the 1950s, '60s, and '70s. People shunned personal adornment, such as jewelry, and if someone had a new jacket or pair of trousers, they would hide it under an old, torn one. The metaphor of the "iron rice bowl" was also part of Maoist philosophy. People were allocated a secure (but low-paid) job for life and an "iron rice bowl" that could never break.

At first the Communists followed their own philosophy—but this self-denial did not last. By the 1960s, sheltered behind high walls, the new emperors were starting to partake of many of the pleasures of life that they did not allow anyone else to enjoy. The official Chinese verdict on Mao nowadays is that, as Deng Xiaoping said, he was "70 per cent good, 30 per cent bad," and that the Cultural Revolution was "a mistake." Nevertheless, his portrait still hangs over the gateway to the Forbidden City, his embalmed body (according to popular rumor, replaced several times by waxworks) occupies a huge mausoleum in Tiananmen Square, and the Chinese still study his teachings, along with "Deng's thought" and "Xi's thought", as part of their formal education. Mao's slogan "The poorer the better" has long been replaced by Deng's much more popular version: "To get rich is glorious." Despite this, it would still be considered inappropriate for a visitor to criticize

Mao, even if some Chinese may do so in private. Public discourse on the subject of Mao is still. In April 2015, a video of a popular CCTV host called Bi Fujian was posted online. Foolishly, he had been filmed insulting Mao at a private dinner party. Mr. Bi apologized, but lost his job—though that is a mild punishment compared to what might have happened a few decades ago.

Yin and Yang

Chinese cosmology sees the universe as being divided into two opposing yet complementary aspects, the primal forces of *yin* and *yang*. Yin corresponds to feminine energy and passivity, as well as earth, moon, cold, and dark, whereas Yang corresponds to active masculine energy, and also heaven, sun, heat, and brightness. The dragon was the embodiment of Yang, and the sun is still known in everyday speech as the Great Yang (*tai yang*). As Yin and Yang alternate, so night is followed by day, and the seasons rotate. The pictorial representation of these polarities is a circle, containing a dark shape surrounding a bright nucleus, and its mirror image. It demonstrates that pure male and female do not exist: each contains its own opposite. This principle of balancing forces is embedded in Chinese philosophy. Everything and everyone are seen as combinations of these complementary and opposing energies. If a family are big believers in Chinese astrology, a baby born on a day considered to have particularly vigorous Yang energy, which is associated with fire, may be given a name which includes a water radical (a radical is a collection of brush strokes in a character that convey a certain meaning, in this case, something related to water, such as "river", or "sea") as a quick way to help balance the child's personality.

Fengshui

Feng is the Chinese word for wind; *shui* means water. It refers to the traditional Chinese belief that there are influences in the natural environment that affect people's fortunes. Every hill, field, and body of water is taken into account in matters such as the siting of graves, temples, homes, and, especially, offices. Since the skill needed for choosing an auspicious site is complex, families or organizations will call in a geomancer, often at considerable expense, before planning decisions are made. Whereas in the West proposals to build new houses or offices on open ground may be objected to on environmental or historical grounds, in southern China villagers still protest against a new building because it would damage the *fengshui* of the area.

PRAGMATISM

The size of the Chinese population and the lack of a social security safety net means that most Chinese are pragmatists. As a result of hardships experienced in the past, the Chinese today have an impassioned focus on the wellbeing of their immediate family and closest friends. A wider sense of community, however, is not nearly as strong. Older generations worked and saved hard to give their children a good education, afford housing, and—if there were any money left over—to travel and enjoy life. Chinese millennials are very much like their counterparts anywhere else in the world—hedonistic, with more disposable income than their parents had and much more to spend it on, hardworking, but also fun loving, and not overly interested in China's bloodstained past. The prized frugality of the past did not rub off on them, and an attitude closer to that of "you only live once," has taken its place, particularly among the so-called Post-90s Generation. They are perhaps the first generation of Chinese who don't have as many hang-ups about borrowing money.

In many ways, however, young people are just as pragmatic as their parents: many choose to pursue university degrees with high earning potential even if their passions lie elsewhere. Yes, some of that decision is due to parental pressure and the importance of filial piety, but a lot of it stems from a simple wish to succeed in China's fiercely competitive environment.

THE CHINESE DREAM

"The Chinese dream," a government catchphrase, was first introduced by premier Xi Jinping shortly after he took office in 2013, and quickly came to replace Hu Jintao's "harmonious society." Over time, however, it has become much more than just an official slogan. The meaning of the phrase was officially translated as "realizing China's national rejuvenation." However, across all levels of Chinese society people have taken the phrase very much to heart and, on the level of the private individual it has inspired people in very similar ways to that of the "American Dream." While large numbers of the wealthy may still look westward, there has emerged a very strong belief that China, too, is a land of opportunity. Anything is possible here, and if you work hard enough, you can change your fate and that of your familys. Life in China's megacities is defined by this spirit of urgency, ambition, and drive to succeed. The race to the top, and all that comes with it—long working hours, little time off, and growing urban alienation—has taken its toll, however. According to one study, one third of under-35s have reported experiencing depression, the causes of which were related to education, career, and one's financial situation.

FACE

The Chinese, like many other Asian nations, are highly sensitive about face—that is, personal reputation or prestige. Any situation where a person is embarrassed, made to look foolish, or not given due respect in front of other people causes loss of face, and can represent a huge blow to one's status. That is why, for example, students in China generally don't jump at the opportunity to ask questions in class or engage in public discussions, though they are becoming more assertive than their parents' generation. If someone cannot answer a difficult question, they may laugh to cover their embarrassment. A person also loses face by becoming angry, upset, impatient, or arguing in public. Phrases like "It is not convenient" or "it is difficult" are often polite code for "no." It is possible to push gently at this seemingly closed door, but don't try to kick it down. For example, if you invite someone to a gathering and they reply that they will think about it, or that they will try their best to make it, the most likely outcome is that they will not show up. Saying so upfront, however, would have made both of you lose face. Criticizing people or poking fun at them (even if it seems good-natured to you) in front of others are other major no-nos.

To Westerners, it may feel the Chinese are wasting time being so indirect; to the Chinese, though, nothing can be more important than preserving relationships and the reputation of everyone involved.

That being said, you can expect many situations where the Chinese will be very direct—and you may wish they weren't—specifically, situations where they don't feel face is jeopardized. For instance, it is normal to ask people if they are single or seeing anyone, or why a married couple still hasn't had a child, or to comment that someone has gotten chubbier. (Indeed, calling someone "fat" is seen as simple statement of fact rather than an insult.)

On the other hand, it may at times be desirable to pay respect through flattery and acknowledgement, especially if there are witnesses. People who have reached a certain social status are not really motivated by money anymore, but they are dead-set on being given the respect they believe they deserve in public. Face is also the answer as to why status items, such as the latest smartphone or designer bags—real, rented, or fake—have become must-haves for a considerable number of Chinese.

ATTITUDES TOWARD THE FAMILY

The family unit is key to every individual's place in
Chinese society. Getting married and producing at least
one child is part of filial duty, and often still not seen as
a matter of personal choice. Children are idolized, which
has bred the phenomenon of "little emperors." It is usual
to find three generations living under the same roof.

Babies and Children

The Chinese adore babies and children; this deep-seated
love of children comes partly from the traditional belief
in the need for family continuity. Westerners traveling
with their children will find them the center of attention.
It can feel a bit overwhelming for Western children—and

their parents! To
most well-meaning
Chinese "aunties"
and "uncles," it
simply will not
occur to them to
ask before pinching
a baby's cheeks or
playing with their
hands. Unsolicited
parenting advice will
be given generously.
On the upside,
however, families
with children will
often receive special

treatment and more attentive service, whether they are
in a local eatery or at the airport.

RESPECT FOR OLD AGE AND ANCESTORS

Another effect of the Confucian emphasis on filial
piety is the respect shown to older people and to more
distant ancestors. Most Westerners have heard vaguely
of the slightly sinister sounding "ancestor worship," but
it simply means showing respect for one's ancestors; the
springtime Tomb-Sweeping Festival (Qingming Jie),
when families bring offerings to the tombs of departed
family members, has regained its traditional importance
after being supressed during Mao's reign. One drawback

of this tradition of venerating old age was, until fairly recently, that anyone who held a position of power was more or less guaranteed to keep the job till he (it usually was a "he") died in office or retired reluctantly at about eighty-five. This did not do much for the country's economy, or the chances of promotion for younger people. But as the free-market economy has taken over, older people are happy enough to retire earlier (China has the lowest mandatory retirement age in the world: sixty for men, and fifty to fifty-five for women). Once their only child has a child or two of their own, they often start a demanding new job—that of full-time child carers.

RESPECT FOR EDUCATION

The Chinese have always valued learning and respected scholars. One of the worst effects of Mao's 1966–76 Cultural Revolution was that a whole generation lost out on schooling. Today, however, 99 percent of primary school-aged children are in education as a result of the free and compulsory nine-year schooling program.

Few in the world are as obsessed with education as Chinese parents, who will go to great lengths to give their children anything that may enhance their competitive edge in today's fast-evolving, knowledge-based economy. In urban areas, families that can afford it part with thousands—sometimes tens of thousands—of yuan every month to pay for their children's education; after-school activities and one-on-one tutoring sessions have gone from luxuries to must-haves, and even relatively modest families will dedicate substantial sums toward their child's education. Teachers and professors are highly respected, though not highly paid.

Parents often lament the academic pressures schoolchildren face; they are often said to have busier schedules than high-flying entrepreneurs. Their days are packed full of classes and they receive enormous amounts of homework. At school, the focus is very much on passing exams, culminating with *gaokao*—China's notoriously tough university entrance exams. Once at university however, students can let out a sigh of relief as the pace and workload become much more manageable.

A general dissatisfaction with the domestic education system means that many families would prefer to send their high school- and university-aged children to study overseas, and growing levels of affluence across society means that more and more are in a financial position to do so. According to the Chinese Ministry of Education, in 2017, more than 600,000 Chinese students left China to study abroad for the first time. The USA, Canada, the UK, Australia, and New Zealand remain the top destinations for studies.

The number of foreign students coming to China is also rising every year. In 2016, over half a million students, hailing largely from South Korea, the USA, Thailand, Russia, and Japan, came to study in China. Most come to learn Chinese, though some study medicine, engineering, finance, and economics.

GUANXI, OR NETWORKING, CHINESE STYLE

Guanxi (connections) has for centuries been the main way of getting anything done—finding a marriage partner, a school or job for your child, a market for your product, a way to cut through red tape, a place to live, or a trip overseas. Nowadays, issues to be solved may be increasingly more complex, but recourse to *guanxi* endures. The first thought a Chinese person may have when presented with a problem they cannot solve themselves may well be, "Who do I know?" On the whole, it was family ties that formed the basis of Chinese *guanxi* because of the moral obligation of relatives to help each other, but anyone you meet and develop relations with can be incorporated into your network. Favors are given and returned in an unspoken web of complex relationships. While foreigners may frown at such pragmatism and feel uncomfortable about mixing the personal and the professional, to the Chinese it is an essential part of life. The foreign visitor to China should be aware of the rules of the *guanxi* game, which, actually, are fairly simple: accepting favors carries an expectation that these will be reciprocated when there is a need. Conversely, doing someone a favor means they will owe you one. In other words, there's no free lunch, and an eye should be kept on the balance of scales. Keep in mind, though, that trying to build *guanxi* by offering expensive gifts or trips abroad could backfire: they may end up being considered a form of bribery by the Chinese government, which has been running fierce anti-corruption campaigns. It could also

become a scenario whereby one may lose face if the
recipient is unable to reciprocate.

ATTITUDES TOWARD RELIGION

China is officially secular, but is tolerant of organized
religions as long as they do not threaten the rule of
the Communist Party. Most Chinese combine a love
of traditions with a practical, materialistic atheism.
But faced with a moral vacuum, as a result of the swift
change from communism to capitalism, organized
religions are growing in popularity; see Chapter 3
for more.

ATTITUDES TOWARD THE STATE

From infancy onward, Chinese education encourages
people to be patriotic, not too questioning of the
Communist Party's hold on power, and to strive to
create a "harmonious society," based on the avoidance
of chaos and the awareness of one's rightful place in
the cosmos. The current government has roped in
Confucius to help keep order, though his ideas were
rejected as feudal under Mao; and, of course, the Party
controls the media at all levels. But even more important
for continued social harmony is the government's ability
to provide food, jobs, housing, health care, and shops
full of everything people could want. As long as all
these boxes are ticked, which they have been during the

period of rapid economic growth, people on the whole are happy to go along with the status quo. Dissident voices are firmly discouraged though, and people tend not to criticize the government openly.

THE MIDDLE KINGDOM: CHINA'S PLACE IN THE WORLD

The Chinese are proud of their country, yet are fairly realistic about its problems, particularly as more and more people study and travel abroad. Ironically, the main evening news bulletin (pre-recorded, as live broadcasts are considered too risky) on China Central TV every evening still focuses on how well China is doing, while broadcasting footage showing that abroad (in other words, on the fringes of empire) people are fighting and killing each other, while suffering from floods, fire, pestilence, and incompetent governments. The format and the message feel about forty years out of date, which is probably why few people take it seriously as a news source any more. China's growing economic and geopolitical influence has allowed the Chinese to shed an inferiority complex stemming from the series of humiliating episodes suffered in the nineteenth century. Even though they may complain among themselves about the country's internal problems, there is also palpable pride at all that China has achieved in the last four decades, as well as at the immense pace it continues to do so. Those born after the 1980s are used to things evolving at increasingly shorter intervals. To them, their counterparts in Western countries often seem too laid back while China, on the other hand, is progressing toward its rightful place—the Kingdom in the middle of it all.

ATTITUDES TOWARD WOMEN

One of the Communists' slow but fairly successful campaigns has been to try and give women in Chinese society more equal rank with men. There is still a traditional preference for sons over daughters, especially in the countryside. When the one-child policy was in effect, this preference led to selective female infanticide, an ancient "feudal" practice, constantly condemned by the government, but which proved surprisingly hard to stamp out. Before ultrasound scans, it was not uncommon in the countryside for an unwanted baby girl to be killed after

我們為參加國家工業化建設而自豪

"We are proud of participating in the founding of our country's industrialization," 1954.

being born. It has led to an imbalance of boys over girls, and today some thirty million men will be unable to find Chinese partners. The law still prohibits doctors and ultrasound technicians from revealing the unborn baby's sex, but in reality, a lot of people end up finding out anyway.

Progress

In 1949, when the Communists took power, the barbaric tradition of binding women's feet to keep them from growing "big and ugly" was still in force, despite earlier efforts to ban it in 1912. As recently as the 1980s, it was common to see elderly ladies with tiny feet hobbling around; thirty years on, that generation has gone.

There have been genuine advances. According to the World Economic Forum's 2018 Global Gender Gap report, China has the world's highest ratio of women in professional and technical jobs, and there are as many female university students as there are male students. However, more education has not translated into higher salaries: on average women receive about one quarter less than their male counterparts who do the same kind of work. Sexual harassment at workplaces and even schools does exist, some of which has been exposed by China's active take on the #MeToo movement, but the vast majority will go unreported. Single mothers remain a particularly stigmatized group, due to having broken both official family planning laws and societal taboos. Likewise, progress for women has been slow in the rarefied atmosphere of Chinese politics. But foreign women traveling in China or working there have nothing to worry about: they will be treated with respect, and on the whole, China is a very safe place for women.

ATTITUDES TOWARD SEX

The widespread availability of contraception and sexual health clinics, plus a general acceptance of women's equality, means that attitudes toward sex are fairly free and easy, though most young Chinese men and women still prefer to date just one person whom they see as a partner for life. China has banned pornography, but not sex stores—you can easily find one of these "adult health stores" in your neighborhood, next to your fruit vendor or your dry cleaner. Prostitution, though technically illegal, is rampant and quietly accepted as part of life—and sometimes, business too. Rows of massage parlors, karaoke bars, and hair salons are not always what they claim to be. Foreign men may find themselves being approached on the street. However, it is in bars and clubs that they should be most careful: women's advances are not usually direct, and so, if it seems too good to be true, it probably is.

Successful Chinese men, including officials, may use sexual relations to demonstrate and enhance their status. It is common for them to keep a mistress—or two, three, or however many they can afford—while staying married. The phenomenon was probably inspired by the historical custom for rich and powerful men to keep concubines, a practice that was definitively banned when the Communists took power. The custom seems to be losing steam among some sections of society, with a number of officials having been forced to drop their mistresses due to anti-corruption campaigns. There still is a whole industry built on adultery, however, including mistress-trainers, and those employed to deter frolicsome husbands by any means necessary.

ATTITUDES TOWARD OVERSEAS CHINESE

Pressure of population, conflicts, and economic woes meant that for centuries there was a steady flow of people leaving China. The earliest emigrants were traders and craftsmen who moved to Southeast Asia, where they continue to play a dominant role in business. In the nineteenth century, laborers or "coolies" (from the Chinese words *ku li*, or "bitter strength") were recruited in large numbers from south China for work in British, French, and Dutch colonies, and in the Americas. By the 1930s, there were nearly ten million overseas Chinese; many have sent money back to their families, invested in factories, and endowed universities in China. The decision to emigrate used to be made principally for economic reasons, and to a lesser extent, political reasons. More recently, however, those emigrating abroad are largely those who have already amassed substantial economic wealth and who are motivated by opportunities in educational advancement and a better quality of life. At the same time, lots of Chinese émigrés—first-, second-, or third-generation—are moving "back" to China, attracted by the country's economic potential. The attitude of the mainland Chinese toward them used to be a toxic mixture of resentment and grudging admiration, but this is less common now. Once back in China, many returnees generally prefer to socialize with those who have also experienced living abroad, or other expats, and rarely mix with mainlanders outside work settings.

ATTITUDES TOWARD FOREIGNERS

Unlike Western societies with their growing cultural diversity, Chinese society is very homogenous; though unequal economically, almost everyone shares a similar racial background. China's National Census in 2010, which was the first one to record expat residents, stated there were at least 600,000 foreigners living in the country. Ten years on, if we are being generous, we can probably guesstimate there to be about 1 million expats, but that would still account for a mere 0.07 percent of the total population. The Chinese use the colloquial term *laowai* (the closest literal translation being "old outsider") to refer to foreigners; some foreigners frown at the word, but in fact the Chinese themselves never consider it derogatory and are surprised that foreigners do.

In China's megacities, foreigners have become such a common sign that they don't excite the same interest they used to just ten years ago. As the Chinese are becoming more confident, unwarranted admiration and an overly reverent attitude toward Westerners are slowly disappearing and are being replaced by a more egalitarian outlook. Although the Chinese tend to keep to themselves and seem to be slow to warm up, they generally enjoy meeting anyone from other countries, of whatever race, and are thrilled to be helpful. Often, it is the language barrier that gets in the way; due to "face" considerations, people may be extra anxious about making mistakes in a foreign language. In remoter regions, an initial wariness is quickly replaced by delighted excitement. This can have its downside for the lone foreigner, who, especially if he or she is traveling with small children, can rapidly start to feel like an exhibit at a freak show—or a minor celebrity. In touristy places, even in cities like Beijing and Shanghai, you may still be approached by someone asking to take photos with or of you—these are often visitors from smaller towns, where foreign faces are uncommon.

From the 1970s onward, many students from Africa came to Chinese universities. Some told of the reaction to their skin color when they walked along the street. Chinese migrant workers from rural areas would come up to them and rub away at their arms, genuinely puzzled, then say "Why don't you go home and wash this coal dust off you?" Today, people of color are usually greeted like any other foreigners, warmly and with interest.

SUPERSTITION

Superstition has stood the test of time well in China. While material life gallops into the future, many traditional beliefs remain intact and are worth being aware of, lest you wonder why, for example, there is no fourth floor in the building you are visiting. In China, numbers are either lucky or unlucky depending on how they are pronounced and which words they sound similar to. Number four, for example, sounds similar to "death" (*si*), and this is why buildings often won't have a fourth floor; nor a fourteenth or twenty-fourth floor for that matter. Western superstition is also sometimes observed, and so the thirteenth floor, too, may be omitted, even though the number has no negative connotations in Chinese. Auspicious numbers include six and nine. Eight, however, is especially lucky—in Chinese it sounds similar to "get rich" (*fa*)! It was for good reason that the Beijing Olympics started on August 8, 2008.

The Chinese zodiac continues to play a role. On years considered lucky (the year of the Dragon, Pig, or Monkey) China experiences a baby boom, with many couples trying for a golden egg.

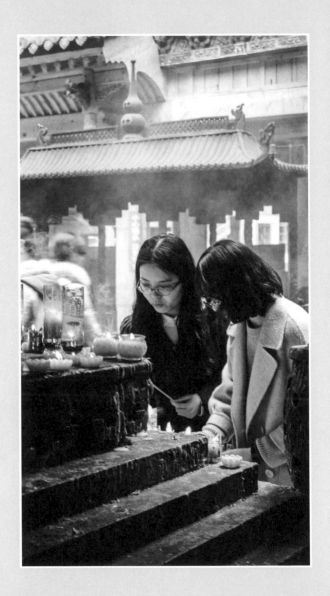

CUSTOMS & TRADITIONS

MANY RELIGIONS AND NONE

For a secular country, China has a large number of religions, five of which are formally recognized: Buddhism, Taoism, Catholicism, Protestantism, and Islam. Confucianism, seen more as a system of thought, has, along with Buddhism and Taoism, shaped Chinese culture profoundly and today has the state's renewed support. What is loosely defined as Chinese "folk religion" contains elements of all three traditions. Islam and Christianity are growing in popularity—a situation that, while tolerated by the ruling Communist Party, is also being closely monitored, regulated, and at times supressed. Practically speaking, freedom of practice is granted, as long it is state-sanctioned and possible to monitor, so as to ensure that no movement is conspiring to overthrow the ruling party, as has happened throughout Chinese history.

Buddhism

One-fifth of China's population identify as Buddhist. In the past, other than in Tibet, where it is the main religion, Buddhism was taken less seriously. Recently, however, as with other aspects of traditional culture, Buddhism has made a major comeback, particularly among the educated urban classes. Brightly painted Buddhist temples are often crowded with people busily "kowtowing" (touching heads to the ground) and lighting incense. There is also often a lot of irreverent laughter and selfie taking.

Islam

Islam is the chief religion in China's northwestern provinces of Xinjiang and Ningxia. Communities of Muslim merchants from Persia and the Arabian

Peninsula are documented to have existed in southern China as far back as the eighth century, during the Tang Dynasty, though traditional accounts describe an Islamic presence a century earlier. While it is thought that only about 1–2 percent of the population today is Muslim, in China that equates to around 20 to 30 million people—no meager sum. In recent years the government has tightened its control over the Muslim population, particularly the Uyghur ethnic minority of Xinjiang, citing the threat of religious extremism.

Christianity

Christianity is China's fastest growing religion. Largely Protestant, the community numbers at about 100 million people, and, if it continues to expand at the current rate (about 7–10 percent annually), by 2030 China will be home to the largest Christian community in the world. Yes, you read that sentence correctly.

A Roman Catholic Church in Yunnan province.

It is perhaps little wonder then that the state, once having treated Christianity with relative tolerance, is today far more active in regulating, and at times restricting and repressing, its churches and communities. Government control in state-sanctioned churches is pervasive. Catholic bishops, for example, are not appointed by the Vatican as is customary, rather they are selected by state-run religious institutions. So-called "house churches," private Christian gatherings, which are common across the country, have always been subject to some degree of repression; nowadays, however, even officially recognized churches are facing suspicion and restriction. Nonetheless, Christianity in China continues to grow. For many, it has stepped in to fill in a moral and spiritual void that has opened up in the transition between two opposing socioeconomic and ideological systems.

Judaism

Jews first came to China in the seventh century during the reign of the Tang dynasty. The most famous Jewish community settled in Kaifeng, Henan province, and for a while were thought to be one of the lost tribes of Israel. Jewish refugees and merchants came to Hong Kong, Shanghai, and Harbin throughout the first half of the early twentieth century. Many of the earliest settlers have been absorbed into the mainstream Chinese population and do not even know of their Jewish ancestry. Nowadays, although China is home to only a few thousand Jews, there has been a rise in interest in all things Jewish or perceived to be Jewish.

HIGH DAYS AND HOLIDAYS

The Chinese use both the same Gregorian calendar as in the West and their own lunisolar calendar, based on precise calculations of the sun's position and the moon's phases. The PRC and the Chinese diaspora follow the lunisolar calendar for traditional festivals and to choose auspicious days for weddings, funerals, moving house, or starting a new business. Unlike in the Gregorian calendar, the same month can be of different lengths in different years. Months begin on the "day of the dark moon" and end the day before the next "dark moon," and the year runs from one winter solstice to the next.

OFFICIAL PRC HOLIDAYS

New Year's Day (Yuandan) January 1

Spring Festival (Chinese New Year, or Chunjie) Usually between late January and mid-February; officially one week off but migrant workers may be off for anywhere between two weeks to a month.

Tomb-Sweeping Day (Qingming Jie) One day off in early April.

Labor Day May 1

Dragon Boat Festival (Duanwu Jie) One day off in early June.

Mid-Autumn Festival (Zhongqiu Jie) One day off in mid to late September.

National Day October 1. Three days off; a lot of people take the week off.

Unless you plan to really go off the beaten path, traveling in China, or anywhere in Asia for that matter, during the national holidays is not advised; tourist destinations are overrun with vacationers, while prices in many popular destinations, such as Thailand or Japan, skyrocket.

Christmas Day is an ordinary working day in China, though it is a holiday in Hong Kong and Macau. Christmas, Chinese style, has been adopted enthusiastically in the big cities, with Santa Claus and shopping as its main rationale; in the countryside and the western areas, where Islam and Buddhism are stronger influences, Christmas is virtually unheard of.

Just as in the West, many holidays are seen by businesses as opportunities to cash in, which perhaps explains the huge popularity of newer additions to the Chinese calendar: Valentine's Day, Mother's Day, Easter, Thanksgiving, Halloween, Christmas, and New Year.

Chinese New Year

Spring Festival, as Chinese New Year is otherwise known, is the most important holiday in China and falls between late January and mid-February. This is the time for family reunions; trains, planes and buses are packed with migrant workers and students heading home. China's new year travel rush is the largest seasonal human migration in the world: in 2019, close to three billion trips took place during this period! Families kick off the celebrations on Chuxi—New Year's Eve—with *nianye fan*, the sumptuous New Year feast. Since 1983, it has also become a tradition for many to watch *Chunwan*, China Central Television's (CCTV) Spring

Public opera performances are a popular feature of New Year celebrations.

Festival Gala, the world's most popular TV program.
(Complaining how much worse the show has become
has also become something of a tradition.) Children and
anyone unmarried are given red envelopes with money.
Nowadays, people send virtual red envelopes with
symbolic amounts of money to each other on WeChat,
China's all-singing, all-dancing super app (see page 188
for more). On the first day of the new year, called *chuyi*,
families gather to make and eat *jiaozi*, stuffed dumplings
shaped like gold ingots to bring good luck. People dress
in new clothes and visit relatives. Younger members
of the family pay respects to the older members (and,
in more traditional homes, to the ancestors as well) by

cupping the fist of one hand in the other in front of their chest upon greeting them. Houses, and especially front doors, are decorated in red, the color of good fortune and happiness. Traditionally, people would set off strings of noisy firecrackers at all hours of the day and night, as well as fireworks, supposedly to scare away evil spirits. In recent years, however, residents have been banned from setting them off in a bid to curb air pollution. New year celebrations are wrapped up two weeks later with Yuanxiao Jie—the Lantern Festival, after which life goes back to normal.

Tomb-Sweeping Day
Tomb-Sweeping Day (Qingming Jie) takes place on the third day of the third month (usually early April), and

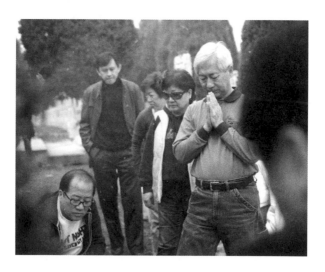

is when families visit the tombs of their ancestors. As part of the visit they will clean the tombstones and make symbolic offerings of joss paper, cooked meats, fish, fruit, and wine. Migrant workers, who may not be able to visit the tombs of departed family members, may simply burn offerings of joss money wherever it is they are located.

Dragon Boat Festival

The Dragon Boat Festival (Duanwu Jie) falls on the fifth day of the fifth lunar month (usually around early June). One story commonly associated with the festival is that of Qu Yuan, an admired poet and minister who committed suicide by jumping into a river when the King of the state refused to listen to his good advice. There are races between long, thin "dragon boats" to the rhythm of drums, said to represent attempts to rescue Qu Yuan. Packets of glutinous rice (*zongzi*) wrapped in leaves are eaten; these are said to have been decoys for the fish so that they would eat the rice rather than devour the hapless Qu Yuan.

Mid-Autumn Festival

Mid-Autumn Festival (Zhongqiu Jie) occurs on the fifteenth day of the eighth lunar month (around mid-September), when the moon is supposed to be brighter than at any other time of the year. It is equivalent to the Western Harvest Festival, and celebrates the reaping of harvest, family reunions, as well as the legend of the moon goddess, Chang'e. Families get together and sit outside around a circular table to admire the full moon and eat "mooncakes," rich round cakes typically stuffed with lotus-seed or sweet bean paste.

"LONELY HEARTS" SHOPPING SPREE

Singles Day, celebrated on November 11, was started in 1993 by male students at Nanjing University as a bachelors' answer to Valentine's Day. The four number ones in the chosen date 11/11 symbolize four "bare sticks," or in other words, lonely singletons. In 2009, China's e-commerce giant Alibaba launched a "shopping festival" to mark the day, which rapidly became the largest retail event in the world. Sales on Singles Day 2019 topped US $38 billion—about five times bigger than Black Friday in the US!

LIFE'S MILESTONES

Births

The birth of a child, particularly a son, is a joyous occasion. During the first thirty days after giving birth the mother would traditionally remain in strict postpartum confinement (called *zuo yuezi*, literally, "sitting the month"): she would not get out of bed, wash her hair, brush her teeth, or even bathe, while religiously following a nutritious postpartum diet. During this time, neither mother nor baby would leave the house, and visitors were not welcome either. The tradition, dating back over a millennium, addresses the new mother's need for recovery and is still very much alive, though bathing and personal care standards have adapted to current understandings of hygiene. Wealthy urban mothers pay anywhere from US $6 to $20 thousand to "sit the month" in style in posh postpartum centers.

After *yuezi* is done, it is time to celebrate: a feast, in which the baby is officially introduced to family and friends, is held one month after birth. Other traditional occasions for a banquet are the baby's one hundred day and one-year birthdays. During the latter, objects symbolizing different occupations are arranged around the baby in a ceremony called *zhuazhou*; whichever object the baby goes for first is believed to indicate their future career. Little fuss is made of subsequent birthdays until the milestone years of sixty, seventy, eighty, and the like, for which large banquets are commonly held. Today, however, younger people celebrate their birthdays in much the same way as their Western counterparts.

Weddings

Weddings in China have always been big, colorful, and expensive occasions. The traditional color for weddings is red, though brides nowadays choose a white Western-style dress for the ceremony and change into a red dress for the banquet. Today, brides and grooms get to choose their own partners; in the past, the family simply chose for them—the bride and groom would often only see each other on the day of the wedding. Before a marriage, a matchmaker would be employed to sort out the details of what was basically a financial transaction, with the groom's family obliged to offer *pinli*, a so-called "bride price." *Pinli* is still very common, even in big cities, and is said to be somewhere around 100,000 yuan (roughly

US $15,000). Nowadays, couples start by registering the marriage, after which it may take a year or longer before they get around to throwing the wedding party. Couples will have elaborate photo shoots months before the wedding, for which many wealthy couples will travel abroad.

The weddings themselves are huge occasions with hundreds of guests. A common complaint among wedding-goers today is that nuptials have become increasingly expensive to attend, and that the material aspect has become somewhat over-emphasised. Depending on the location and your relationship with the couple, you may be expected to give anywhere from one hundred to a thousand dollars.

Funerals

Traditionally, the color white, which symbolizes death and grief, was worn at funerals. Nowadays, however, dark colors are also worn. A dark piece of cloth may also be pinned to the sleeves of those who attend by a close relative of the deceased. If the deceased has made it to seventy years old, there is not thought to be any reason for serious grief, though there will be a lot of ritual lamentation—often by professional mourners—during the funeral procession. Entire shops are devoted to selling paper money, paper furniture, cars, houses, and paper clothes—anything the departed may need in the afterlife—that are burned and placed with the body on burial. Even the non-religious will often pay a Buddhist or Daoist priest to say prayers and perform ceremonies for the soul of the dead person.

Traditionally the Chinese believed that the body had to go into the next world intact or its ghost would never be at peace, so cremation used to be unpopular (organ donation even more so); today, however, cremation in many cities has become compulsory. Around 10 million people die every year, and there simply is not enough space to bury them all: the price of a tomb in Shanghai, for example, starts from around US $10 thousand. Some years ago the ever-practical Chinese government began offering a new pathway to the afterlife to help ease the demand for land plots: state subsidized sea burial. The chosen day for these mass burials at sea is the Qing Ming holiday, the traditional day for tomb sweeping and ancestor visiting, and they are becoming more popular.

TRADITIONAL CHINESE MEDICINE

Enter even the most modern-looking pharmacy in China and you will notice that it is divided into two different sections: "Western Medicine," and "TCM," which stands for Traditional Chinese Medicine. TCM is often still the first choice for the majority of Chinese when treating common ailments such as a cold, a runny nose, or various stomach complaints. Therefore, if you have the flu and are looking for something along the lines of Tylenol, make sure to stress that you are after "Western medicine" or you will be given vials of ready-to-drink TCM herbal tincture. TCM is much more than tinctures, however; it is a whole collection of holistic health management and wellbeing practices that encompass acupuncture, moxibustion (burning medicinal herbs close to the skin), *tuina* (a therapeutic massage), cupping, diet, *tai chi*, and *qigong*.

TCM is a complex system that has developed over some 2,300 years and is based on the understanding that the body is a cosmos in miniature. From this perspective, illness is a reflection of disharmony in the flow of *qi* (vital energy) through the body's meridian pathways. Heavily influenced by Taoism, it incorporates concepts such as *yin* and *yang*, and the five elements. It stresses prevention first and foremost, and its wisdom often leaves Westerners perplexed: how are tangerines causing excessive "internal heat" and what does it have to do with my acne? To most Chinese, much of this is simply common knowledge.

Chinese medicine hospitals exist throughout the country; housed in large modern complexes, they are a far cry from the obscure-looking TCM shops you might be used to seeing at home.

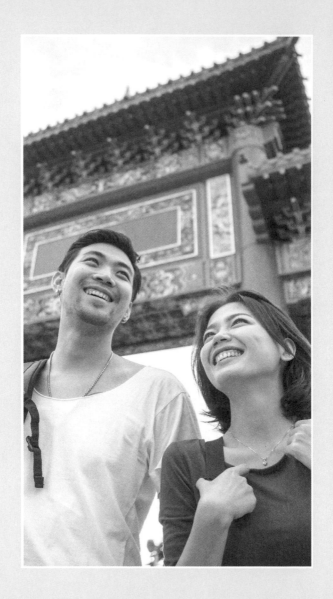

CHAPTER FOUR

MAKING FRIENDS

FRIENDSHIPS

Friendships with Chinese people are, perhaps contrary to a visitor's expectations, relatively easy to form and can last a lifetime. The number of foreign residents in China is reckoned at over 850,000—a tiny percentage of the huge population. This is not counting tourists, of whom there were about 30.5 million in 2018, according to Chinese government figures. So as a foreigner you will likely have scarcity value, and if you make a small effort to meet and befriend local people, they will be only too pleased. Whether it is through work, while backpacking, through going out to bars, concerts, or clubs, or through dating or the Internet, you can build friendships with locals quite easily.

Though perhaps a little shy initially, people in China are usually very friendly and helpful, and many will feel it is their duty to look out for you on their home turf. Many are also only too happy to practice their English, get ideas about traveling or working overseas, and generally just experience talking to someone from another, non-Chinese, world. As anywhere else, lasting friendships boil down to personal chemistry, but the opportunity is most certainly there for the taking.

A word to the wise: centuries of living under a capricious central state means people rely on each other more than any external power, so the bonds of friendship are taken seriously, and you must not let your new friends down. The Chinese are sincere and steadfast in their friendships; they may not see someone very often, but the relationship will prevail over the course of years regardless. Close friends are seen as family. You can count on your Chinese friends to be there for you in time of need, and the same will be expected of you. In friendships with the opposite sex, tread carefully if you prefer to keep them platonic—friendliness can sometimes be misinterpreted as romantic interest.

Most visitors to China tend to mix socially with urban, middle-class Chinese, who have more in common with the average Westerner than with the rural inhabitants of their own country. In Beijing, Shanghai, and Shenzhen, many people will speak fairly good English, particularly those under forty; however, you may feel that in large cities, like elsewhere in the world, people sometimes prefer to keep to themselves. Outside the megacities, the locals will express an interest in getting to know you much more directly, but conversation may be limited because of the language barrier. Even if you learn enough Mandarin to carry on a conversation, some regional dialects can be pretty impenetrable.

MEETING AND GREETING

On meeting someone, of either sex and any age apart from very young children, the usual practice is to give a little nod with a smile, wave, or in more formal settings, shake hands—often for a much longer time than would be usual in the West. If you go for the latter, make sure to shake hands with everyone you are meeting. For the introduction, stand up and stay upright until invited to sit or until others have begun sitting down. When in doubt in China, err on the side of formality, or take your cue from your Chinese counterparts.

Upon meeting someone new, you may be asked questions that in many Western countries would be considered personal, such as "Are you married?", "Are you in a relationship?", "Do you have any children?", or even "How much do you earn?" If you prefer not to answer directly, then you can deflect the questions with good humor.

INVITATIONS HOME

In cities, it is much more common to meet friends and entertain guests outside the home. With restaurants of all kinds being both ubiquitous and affordable, hosting guests at home is often seen as an unnecessary hassle. That said, if you are invited for a home-cooked meal, you should feel honored, as such a privilege usually befalls only the closest family friends.

Invitations home are usually for a weekend lunch or, less commonly, dinner. Upon your arrival, you will be offered slippers kept especially for guests. In the cities, you will never see the Chinese wear shoes inside the home. That being said, the Chinese dread being barefoot, so offering slippers to guests is considered an indispensable courtesy.

Often, if it is a three-generations-under-one-roof kind of household, the cooking will be done by the grandparents; less commonly, by a domestic helper. In cities today it is so cheap, fast, and convenient to have any kind of food delivered that it is a popular option for many who are entertaining. They may even use an app to book a chef to come in and do the cooking. The meal is unlikely to be a fancy affair. The dining table is sure to be covered with dishes, but the food itself will not be different from what the family would usually eat on any given day. This itself is as a sign of closeness to be appreciated: the less Chinese people stand on ceremony with you, the closer they consider you to be.

Your hosts, particularly if they are older, may well fuss over how much you are not eating; the genial urging simply means they have adopted you as their own. Hosts may even pick up pieces of food and put it in your bowl—the ultimate sign of affection. Although using serving spoons and chopsticks has become increasingly common in many families, people may still use their own chopsticks to pick up food directly from sharing plates. If alcohol is served, don't be surprised to find your glass filled almost to the brim; as with the number and sizes of dishes, when it comes to showing hospitality, for the Chinese, the more, the better.

GIFT GIVING

The Chinese see home gatherings as extremely casual occasions among the nearest and dearest, and so bringing gifts is nice but not a must, unless you are coming on a holiday, such as Chinese New Year. If there are children, a nice gesture would be to bring them a small toy. Otherwise, anything foreign— especially alcohol, chocolates, or snacks—will be appreciated. A nicely packaged fruit basket is a safe bet for any occasion. Foreign or premium brand cigarettes used to be the most coveted gift, but with attitudes toward smoking shifting in the cities, it is best to check ahead. In the countryside, a carton of expensive cigarettes will still make you a star guest, even if the hosts are not smokers—they can always re-gift the cigarettes.

During the New Year festival, go big: large boxes of snacks or tea beautifully packaged in red, or bottles of alcohol will be welcomed. The gifts themselves don't need to be pricey, but make sure they are a good size and nicely packaged. For formal or business-related occasions, you can also bring artwork typical of your country or souvenirs.

Some Dos and Don'ts

Do not give your Chinese friends a clock, as the word for clock sounds similar to "attend upon a dying parent." Other gifts to avoid are sharp objects, symbolizing the end of a friendship; handkerchiefs, usually reserved for the end of a funeral; pears, because the word *li*, sounds like "parting"; yellow chrysanthemums and any white flowers, as they too are seen at funerals; umbrellas, *san* in Chinese sounding similar to "breaking up"; and mirrors, which are believed to attract ghosts. Wrap presents in red, gold, or yellow, and avoid white.

Don't spend large sums on personal gifts to friends—
they may be embarrassed if they are not able or ready
to reciprocate. Make sure to offer the gift with both
hands and say something along the lines of "I got you a
little something, it's really nothing much." The Chinese
will often refuse your gift at least once and up to as
many as three times before accepting. Older people
may sometimes physically push the present away and
scold you for wasting money—refusing gifts at first is
to express that it is your relationship that matters, not
material objects. That is also why the recipient of the
gift will most likely not open it in front of you, instead
quickly putting it away.

TIMEKEEPING

Whether joining a new friend for a meal, going to an
old friend's house, or taking part in a business meeting,
punctuality is important. The Chinese consider it rude
to be late. Chinese people rise early and go to bed early,
so lunch will probably be anywhere between 11:30 a.m.
to 1:00 p.m. and evening meals are likely to begin around
6:00 p.m. Meals, meetings, and visits end promptly. Once
the meal is over, the guests will chat for a few minutes but
should then get up and go. If you are a guest at someone's
home, it is fine to stay a bit longer to avoid a departure
that feels abrupt. It is polite for your hosts to accompany
you all the way to the exit or to the elevator, or to see
you into your taxi to say good-bye. The Chinese way to
reciprocate would be to urge them to go back inside.

MEN AND WOMEN

If you are dealing with someone of the opposite sex, there is unlikely to be any physical contact after the initial handshake, but members of the same sex do tend to touch each other more than in the West, especially women. It is rare for people to kiss friends. Though hugging is becoming more common, a lot of people still prefer limited physical contact with people other than their romantic partner.

Dating
Usually when a Chinese couple starts dating, it is automatically assumed that the relationship is serious

and may lead to marriage; once they introduce each other to their parents, marriage is almost guaranteed. Visiting Westerners who date Chinese people should be aware of this—what they may see as a casual affair is likely to be taken much more seriously by their Chinese partner, who may expect that what for them is a "serious" love affair will lead to marriage. Simply put, Chinese people don't date casually.

Other than that, there are no special rules to follow, except to remember that social drinking plays a much less important role in Chinese society (especially for women), and that young Chinese women expect to be treated with a more old-fashioned sense of chivalry than their Western counterparts. By default, it is the guy who picks up the bill in restaurants and elsewhere. In China, splitting the bill is not accepted in any kind of setting—romantic, platonic, or professional—but even less so on dates. A man would feel a tremendous loss of face if he wasn't allowed to pay.

When Western women date Chinese men, they usually say that they are kind and considerate. They will often have been educated to think of women as equals, or even as superiors, since there is a shortage of marriageable women, on top of which Chinese women are now outperforming men at school and university. They will also still insist on pampering their date the old-fashioned way. Regional stereotypes about men are still strong: the men in the north of China are said to be more macho and traditional, while southerners are supposedly softer and often take care of the housework and cooking.

Gay China

Homosexuality in China was legalized in 1997 and removed from classification as a mental illness in 2001. In recent years attitudes toward the LGBT community have become much more relaxed. In big cities, the extremely androgynous look, especially for women, has become somewhat common; no one bats an eyelid anymore. Major cities have active LGBT scenes, and young gay people often come out to their friends and, in many international companies, to their colleagues too. However, many will not come out to their families. The Confucianist value of filial piety prevails, and many are under pressure from their parents to marry and produce at least one child. This has led most gay people to remain in the closet among family, enter into fake marriages, and look for other creative solutions, such as finding friends or paying people to pose as their opposite sex partner in front of their parents.

SENSITIVE TOPICS

In private, and once people know and trust you, they will talk freely. However, it is best to avoid discussing politics, especially the "three Ts": Tibet, Taiwan, and Tiananmen Square. Tibet is seen as an integral part of China, and any foreigner discussing its independence is met with bewilderment. Mention of the second "T," Taiwan, is equally futile; and few young people in China know what actually happened in Beijing's Tiananmen Square in 1989, when popular protests were brutally suppressed by the army. Any discussion of the event online, including using related keywords, has been banned for years. While you may take your cue from whoever you are talking to about which topics are off-limits, bear in mind that while a person might be outspoken on domestic issues, they may yet be embarrassed, and possibly defensive, if a foreigner were to do the same.

CHINESE NAMES

In China the surname precedes the personal name, since the family group or clan is more important than the individual. Zhang Hua is thus Mr. Zhang, not Mr. Hua. Only thirty surnames have two syllables; the rest are of one syllable only, and some of the commonest are Zhang, Wang, Wu, Zhao, and Li.

When addressing the Chinese people you meet it is best to use Mr., Ms., Miss, plus their surnames: Chinese people are more formal than many Westerners. The all-purpose title used by the Communists, *Tongzhi*, or "Comrade," has long dropped out of use. It is not usual to address Chinese women as Mrs., as they don't change their names after marriage.

The Chinese often refer to one another by job titles, such as Mayor Wang, Manager Li, Teacher Zhang, and so on; it is a useful habit to adopt. If you are working in China, they may well refer politely to you in the same way.

Those with one syllable first names should be addressed using both first and family names, including among family, friends, and colleagues. For example, Yang Huan would never just be called Huan—that would be considered rude no matter what the personal relationship is. On the other hand, if the person's first name is longer—made up of two syllables, as in for example Xueli of Yang Xueli—it is possible to call this person simply Xueli if you are close in age and once you know each other well. When in doubt, stick to full names.

Nowadays, a lot of urban Chinese are adopting English names, not just to make things easier for Western colleagues, but also to use among themselves, regardless of whether they speak English or not.

"Everyman"

An affectionate nickname for ordinary Chinese people is *lao bai xing*, or "old hundred names." Government figures show that the most popular one hundred surnames actually cover nearly 85 percent of China's population. In all there are some 4,000 Chinese surnames, but that is still an incredibly small number considering the size of the population.

Similarly, foreigners residing in China often adopt Chinese names and will use them in their daily interactions. The sound and meaning of a name are important in China. If you can find someone to help you think up a good Chinese name, your business card will have more impact.

Another acceptable way of addressing people is to use their surname and the word *xiao* or *lao* in front of it. *Xiao* means "little" or "young"; *lao* means "old." The cut-off point is around thirty-five; so if you are a foreigner who starts visiting China when you are still *Xiao* Smith, one day you will have to get used to being called *Lao* Smith. Just remember that the Chinese are showing respect for your advancing age, even though you had rather hoped no one would notice it. *Lao*, however, can also be used as a term of endearment between friends.

Using *xiao* and *lao* is acceptable among friends and colleagues, but not for someone you don't know well. If you are addressing your Chinese friends' parents or other relatives around the same age as your parents, you can call them uncle—"*shushu*," or auntie—"*ayi*."

Ms. Hu and Mr. Li

Women in China, with the exception of Hong Kong and Macau, do not change their surnames when they marry, so it could take a while before you realize that Ms. Hu and Mr. Li are actually married! A child normally takes the father's surname, but if the couple has two children, one may take the father's and the other the mother's. Some families will combine both.

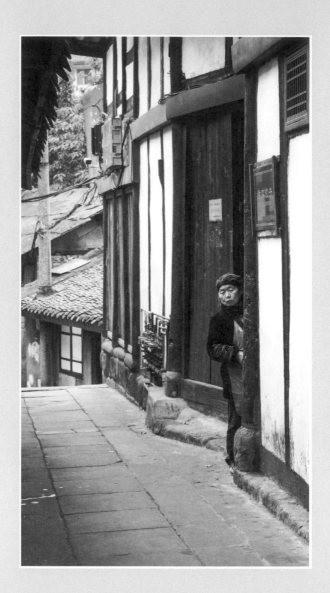

CHAPTER FIVE

PRIVATE *&* FAMILY LIFE

THE FAMILY UNIT

In China, the traditional family has for centuries been regarded as the basis of society and of the individual's guarantee of happiness and security. While much has changed in China in recent decades, this largely has not. Rigid rules about premarital sex have relaxed, but unmarried mothers are rare. Divorce rates, though traditionally low, are rising, and looking after elderly family members at home rather than exiling them to an old people's "home" is almost universal.

In southern China especially, the family is often part of a much larger clan, whose duty is to help each other. Children are expected to show respect to their parents; this is the fundamental concept of filial piety as defined by Confucius. Some commentators feel that the one-child policy has had a negative effect on filial piety, creating several generations of children who are worshiped by their adoring parents, and who, because they have no siblings, have not had to learn the tedious

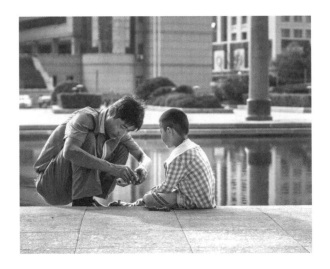

early lessons of sharing. The Chinese have dubbed these children "little emperors," and they can be seen everywhere practicing "pester power," that is, getting their parents to buy them things. However, much of this is just down to the Chinese love of small children; by the time the little emperors start school, being an only child puts them under considerable pressure to fulfil singlehandedly all their family's hopes.

In the remoter rural areas, family life is less focused on the needs of one small person, and more on the need of the whole household to pull together to create wealth (or just to survive). The importance of the extended family is reflected in the language: Chinese has a host of kinship terms for every family member, indicating whether the person is from the mother's or father's side, and their order of birth in the family. For instance, the term for an uncle who is the mother's older brother is different from that of an uncle who is the father's younger brother, and who is also the youngest of four children.

The first generation of singletons still had cousins and would refer to them using terms reserved for siblings, so if someone under the age of forty is telling you about his or her brother or sister, they probably have a cousin in mind.

Those born more recently under the one-child policy often won't have any uncles, aunts, or cousins to speak of, but they may have hope for a sibling: in 2015, in a bid to stem the potentially catastrophic economic fallout of an aging population the government doubled the number of children permitted per couple to two. So far, however, the policy has largely failed to bring about the desired change. According to the National Bureau of Statistics, two million fewer babies were born in 2018 compared with the previous year. Reluctance to have a second child is especially strong in the cities. With parents spending exorbitant amounts on education and other needs, many say they simply can't afford a second child. Other than the financial burden, there are also reservations about the quality of life in cities, the lack of helping hands, hesitation on the part of working mothers to put their careers on hold again, and, last but certainly not least, the lifestyle of a single-child family has now become familiar and the status quo. The typical urban family unit therefore will usually consist of parents, a single child, and one set of grandparents, who double up as child carers while the parents are at work.

HOUSING

With the rapid demolition of many of the traditional courtyard homes that made cities like Beijing so attractive in the past, most Chinese now live in high-rise apartment blocks. The PRC has severe housing problems, despite a massive amount of construction. Limited space means homes often look cluttered, with every inch of space used for storage. People live on top of each other with little privacy. Conflicts are common over minor issues—a playful child, a noisy television.

Apartment prices, especially in the megacities of Beijing, Shanghai, and Shenzhen, are notoriously high. According to the *South China Morning Post*, homes in Beijing that sold for an average of around 4,000 yuan (US $580) per square meter in 2003, were worth more than 60,000 yuan (US $8,600) per square meter in 2018. Zhang Lin, an independent commentator, pointed out that an average household would have to work for more than two decades, without spending, to afford a home in Beijing today—almost twice as long as in New York or Tokyo. Although renting works out much cheaper overall, people still go out of their way—and outside their means—to become home owners. According to Forbes, 90 percent of families in China own their home. Often, the savings of the whole extended family are put toward the down payment for a city property. It seems as though foreign experts are forever busy predicting the burst of China's property bubble. So far though, it remains intact.

In the countryside, farming families also tend to own their homes, and whenever they have some spare cash, they build another room, or a whole new story. But as more young people move away for work, the traditional extended family is starting to break up.

SOCIAL RELATIONS AND OCCUPATIONS

The number of graduates in China continues to grow at an impressive rate. Indeed, there are now ten times as many as there were just two decades ago. One unfortunate effect of this development, however, is that competition for suitable jobs has now become incredibly fierce; entry-level positions for university graduates can sometimes be lower paid than those of low-skilled laborers. On paper, China has a standard forty-hour, Monday-to Friday work week; however, those in private companies who wish to speed up their careers often put in a lot more than that and without being compensated. China's tech companies operate a notorious though unwritten rule referred to as "966," meaning workers are expected to work from 9:00 a.m. to 9:00 p.m., Monday to Saturday. A six-day work week is common in the service industry too, and conditions among migrant workers sometimes being worse still. Even the so-called "sea-turtles"—a pun referring to graduates of overseas universities who return to China—are not having an easy time of it: fresh graduates earn on average around US $710 (5,000 yuan) a month—far from enough to live comfortably in China's increasingly expensive megacities.

DAILY LIFE

The Chinese rise early, around 6:00 a.m., and are often at work or school by 7:30 a.m. The journey to work in big cities is hard, as all roads and all forms of transportation are packed. From childhood onward, at school and at work, many people have a short nap after lunch and find it hard to function if they don't. The Chinese have been known for their ability to sleep anywhere, anytime, and that includes at their desktop.

People usually finish work or school around 6:00 p.m. and buy food for the evening meal on the way home from supermarkets, street markets, or online vendors who will deliver the food to their door within half an hour. Otherwise, either men or women may do the cooking at home. In large cities though, it is often a domestic helper who prepares the meals: as many as one fourth of Shanghai families employ an *ayi* ("auntie") who will take care of everything from cooking to childcare. Evening meals out are also popular and affordable.

EDUCATION

The school year begins in September; students have their winter holidays from around mid-January to the end of February, their summer holidays from July to the end of August. Their lives are much more regulated than in the West, with even very young children having responsibilities such as that of classroom monitor; these duties are taken very seriously. Children often stay late at school with their teachers to make a start on their homework, of which they have a huge amount, or attend various afterschool tutorials and other extracurricular activities. Taking extra classes in Chinese, English, and math is the norm, as is learning to play a musical instrument, a source of valuable extra points for the *gaokao*, university entrance exams. Discipline is strict, with much rote learning. Class sizes are big. This regime continues right up to university, with highly competitive exams at every stage.

In a bid to help their child stay on top, families who can afford to will buy housing around so-called "key schools," so as to improve their chances of gaining admission. Obviously, house prices in these areas are very high. Parents are mostly fiercely supportive of

schools; teachers and parents are in touch daily.
In all, parents spend a lot of time pushing and
encouraging their children, as well as working hard
themselves in order to save money so that they may
afford to put them through university.

Rural children have it much harder. Often referred
to as the "left-behind" children, as their parents have
migrated to the cities in search of employment, these
children are mostly cared for by their grandparents
and have to contend with issues their urban
counterparts do not, such as completing household
chores in addition to their studies. With limited
education opportunities it is getting harder for these
children to compete academically with their peers
from the cities.

THE THIRD AGE

At least one sector of the population has a rather less
stressful life—older people can relax, look after their
grandchildren, go to the park to dance, sing, or do
taijiquan, travel, and know that they are respected
and loved by their families. Universities for seniors
are booming, too. Life can be tougher for those in the
countryside though, where social benefits are more
limited, and the elderly rely more heavily on their
children and family for support.

On the whole, people are living longer, healthier
lives. In light of falling birth rates, however, this
otherwise positive development constitutes part

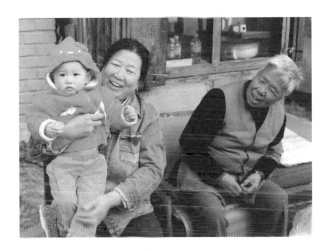

of a much larger issue facing China's economy: a population that is living longer, with fewer young people to shoulder the burden.

LOVE AND MARRIAGE, OR NOT

The parents of today's young Chinese men and women had to get the permission of their superiors in their *danweis* (work units) to get engaged, married, or divorced. This was in part an attempt to stop the forced early marriages of old China; the minimum age for getting married, or even dating, was set at around twenty-five, which was also a way of controlling population growth. Things are freer now and it is more common to live together before marriage; the problem

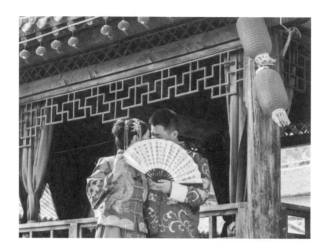

for young couples (as in the West) is a shortage of affordable accommodation. The legal age of marriage today is twenty for women and twenty-two for men. In rural areas, young people are often expected by their families to marry as soon as legally possible, while in the cities most will only tie the knot in their late twenties or early thirties. In recent years, a trend of "flash marriages" has emerged, whereby a couple will get married within a hundred days of first meeting—a response perhaps to the pressure to settle down once the years of initial career building have passed.

In the past, a happy marriage was rare; the husband's mother was often cruel to the new bride, who rarely left the house. Widows did not remarry, as it was thought immoral to marry more than once. Since 1949, the legal position of women has improved considerably: however, the equality pendulum is swinging back. The derogatory phrase "leftover women" has been coined by the Party to describe Chinese women who are still unmarried at the ripe old age of twenty-eight. According to a book on the topic by American academic Leta Hong Fincher, in 2011 China's official Xinhua news agency published an editorial saying that: "The tragedy is women don't realize that as they age they are worth less. . . , so by the time they get their M.A. or Ph.D., they are already old, like yellowed pearls." Dr. Hong Fincher writes: "The government believes that society is more stable with fewer single people; new families drive consumption and the property boom. Plus, if educated females are married, then 'better quality' children will be born." Despite the official revival of this age-old social stigma, today's highly educated women are no longer easy to browbeat, and are fighting back. Some have taken a different word, similar to "leftover" in Chinese, but which means "triumphant," and are using it to describe themselves and their decision to stay single.

When women do marry, they no longer feel obliged to stay that way. Rates of divorce have grown every year since 2003, when the process was simplified and made cheaper. In Beijing, 40 percent of marriages now end in divorce. Some say social media has made love affairs easier, while others acknowledge that women now expect more, and will no longer put up with domestic violence or a cheating husband. They also earn more now, and no longer need a husband to pay the bills. The stigma of divorce has gone—and, surprisingly, only costs a few RMB plus about half-an-hour's time to fill out the paperwork.

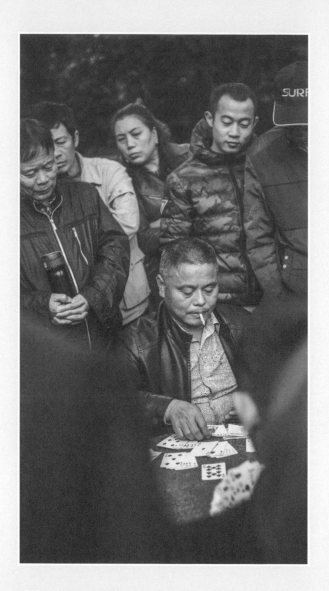

CHAPTER SIX

TIME OUT

Working hours in China are longer than in the West, and people, by and large, are dedicated to their careers. Though free time may be a precious commodity, people today have more ways to spend it, and will usually try to make the most out of it. Popular pasttimes include eating out with friends, playing and watching sports, shopping, taking classes, going to cinemas and concerts, clubs and karaoke bars. As a visitor, all these pastimes are open to you, as participant or spectator. A lot of people's free time is also often spent online, whether keeping up on social media, gaming, livestreaming shows, or playing with the latest video or beautification app.

All the major cities have English-language Web sites giving information on what's on locally, and Chinese friends, colleagues, and tour guides will be happy to tell you more, or accompany you.

Chinese tourism is increasing year on year. Domestic travel is hugely popular—being generally inexpensive it is enjoyed by most, particularly on public holidays. For those who can afford it, foreign destinations in

Asia, Europe, the US, and Australia are popular, and there is a growing niche for roads less traveled: Africa, the Caribbean, and even Antarctica, to name a few. Perhaps almost as important as the trip itself are the accompanying photographs and clips uploaded and shared across the various social media platforms; foreign travel continues to confer social status, and the posts they generate are a valuable form of social currency.

EATING IN AND OUT

From roadside vendors in nondescript backstreets to upscale restaurants in heaving city centers, China's passion for food is omnipresent. Between the traditional and the innovative, the sheer variety in local cuisines is reason enough for any self-respecting foodie to make their way here at once. Not to put too fine a point on it, the Chinese take their food very seriously: in large cities, people will drive across town and stand in line for hours just to taste (and probably also photograph!) the latest dessert or milk tea variation. Neither is it unusual for people to think twice about traveling or moving abroad, perturbed by the simple question: "But what will I eat over there?"

The traditional Chinese diet has many vegetables, with food cooked fast so that the goodness is not destroyed. Shopping for food is done with gusto and everything is prodded, shaken, sniffed, and thoroughly examined before being purchased. Few Chinese eat "ready meals"; food is freshly cooked for each meal, and

fish, meat, and poultry are often killed only a short time before they are cooked. In restaurants you often choose your fish from a selection swimming in a huge tank.

Only a few decades ago, Chinese people still largely subsisted on a diet that consisted primarily of starchy foods, such as wheat noodles in the north, or rice in the south, alongside some vegetables. Meat or fish were rare luxuries; beef, for example, used to be called "millionaire's meat." Today that is all a distant memory—most people can, and do, consume meat (mostly pork, but also chicken and beef) on a daily basis; staples such as rice or noodles, meanwhile, remain integral and non-negotiable.

On the whole, food in mainland China will look, smell, and taste somewhat different from what Westerners are used to in Chinese restaurants back at home. The variety can be overwhelming at first: there are all kinds of dumplings, hotpot, vegetable, meat and seafood dishes, and so much more. Some of it, however, may be less appealing to Western tastes, such as hundred-year-old eggs, sea cucumbers, salted eels, donkey stew, spicy duck heads, and chicken feet, to name a few. If you are seized by a desire for familiar food, in large cities, well-known fast-food outlets are ubiquitous; you will find cuisine from every corner of the world in the megacities, with Shanghai's dining scene on a par with the world's best.

In many restaurants, bars, and clubs in today's China you could be anywhere in the modern world; venues are fashionably sleek, quiet, and clean. Out in the real world, however, and even sometimes at banquets, things are a bit more down to earth. The Chinese enjoy a bit of *renao*, noise and bustle—it is an integral part of sharing a meal. There is not much in the way of etiquette in simple eateries, where noisy eating and loud slurping is commonplace and not considered rude. At more formal venues and events, however, it is rather a different story.

Restaurant Etiquette
When you arrive at a more upmarket restaurant, staff will rush forward and guide you to a table. Do not worry if you cannot read Chinese; even if the menu is not in English, it should have pictures of the main

dishes, or you can always point to what someone else is eating. The staff will be very attentive and will pour out tea, arrange a clean linen napkin on your lap as though you were a child, and generally fuss over you. You will be asked about your dietary restrictions (*jikou*) and most restaurants will do their best to accommodate your needs. However, do be careful if you have serious allergies—peanuts and peanut oil, for instance, are widely used.

It is the host who usually does the ordering, though other guests are welcome to chime in too. Meals are shared from communal plates, from which everyone serves themselves. Use the serving chopsticks and spoons to put food onto your plate; in more upscale restaurants, white chopsticks are for serving yourself from the communal plates, while black ones are for eating with (don't worry, it's no great sin if you get them mixed up.)

Try to taste a bit of everything, but pace yourself, as there is probably more food coming than you might be used to. Food is often served in the following order: cold dishes, hot dishes, staple foods, and soup, followed by dessert or fruit.

In China's collectivist and *guanxi*-based culture, where face, honor, and dignity are preeminent values, splitting the bill is among the more incomprehensible of Western customs. Here, whoever initiated the meal is expected to treat the whole party. You may politely offer to pay, but don't be surprised when your offer is turned down. If your invitation was not part of requesting a favor or saying thanks for one, then you can reciprocate by inviting and picking up the bill next time.

TIPPING

Tipping is generally not part of the culture in China, though there are exceptions. If you leave a tip at a restaurant and walk out, in most cases, you will be chased after by the staff with the money that you have "forgotten." One exception is upmarket hotels, where it is usual to tip the bellboy and other staff. High-end restaurants usually include a 15 percent service charge in the bill; and if service is not included, it is not necessary to tip. If you book a car using a ride-hailing app or order food on one of the delivery apps, it is possible to offer a virtual tip upfront so that your order is picked up faster, or as a thank-you for good service. A tip of 10-30 yuan, either in cash or in a virtual red envelope on WeChat, will be gladly received. In Hong Kong and Macau, tip as you would in the West.

REGIONAL CUISINE

Chinese local dishes are said to belong to four, or eight, or ten culinary schools, depending on who you believe. Canton, Shandong, Sichuan, and Yangzhou make up four; Hunan, Fujian, Anhui, and Zhejiang make eight; include Beijing and Shanghai, and you have ten. You could also add the Middle Eastern influenced cooking of the Hui and Uyghur people,

whose roadside stalls produce wonderful (and cheap)
lamb kebabs and naan bread.

Cantonese Food

Cantonese food is widely considered the pinnacle of
Chinese cuisine. It uses a wide range of ingredients;
there is a Chinese saying that "The Cantonese will
eat anything with wings, except a plane, and anything
with four legs, except a table." River and seafood are
widely used, and you may even find rats and insects
on the menu. Some of the more esoteric dishes
are "three kinds of snake stewed," cat meat, stewed
mountain turtle, and crispy skin suckling pig.

Shandong Food

Shandong lies on a peninsula, so its cuisine is dominated
by seafood. Dishes include sea cucumber with scallion,
stewed snakehead eggs, and sea slugs with crab ovum.

Sichuan Food

Sichuan cuisine is renowned for its hot, peppery flavor. The Sichuanese use a special black pepper that leaves the lips numb—not unpleasant when one grows accustomed to it. The variety of tastes is summed up in the phrase "a hundred dishes with a hundred flavors." Dishes include shredded pork with fish flavor, stewed bean curd with minced pork in pepper sauce, and dry-roast rock carp.

Huaiyang Food

Huaiyang cuisine integrates the best of dishes in Yangzhou, Zhenjiang, Huaian, and other places south of the Yangtze River, stressing "freshness and tenderness, careful preparation, cutting skill, bright color, beautiful arrangements, and delicate flavoring" according to one enthusiast. Famous dishes include beggar's chicken, fried mandarin fish with sweet and sour sauce, and minced pork balls in a casserole.

Vegetable Dishes

Vegetable dishes have been popular since the Song dynasty (960–1279). They were divided into three schools: Monastery Vegetable Dishes, Court Vegetable Dishes, and Folk Vegetable Dishes. Ingredients include green leaved vegetables, fruit, edible mushrooms, and bean curd cooked in vegetable oil. Vegetarians and vegans don't always have it easy in today's China, however—many vegetable dishes may still be flavored with slices of fatty pork and the like. A selection of *chunsu* (vegan) and *sushi* (vegetarian) eateries, both Chinese and Western, are readily available in the big cities, and if not, you should be able to find simple vegetarian meals nearby Buddhist temples.

DRINKS

The Chinese drink large quantities of green tea, without milk or sugar. Tea is drunk constantly at meetings, at work, in restaurants, and at formal meals. It is usually served in mugs with lids to keep it warm. Teabags and tea strainers are not used, and drinking tea without swallowing a mouthful of soggy tea leaves requires concentration: try using the lid as a strainer when sipping.

Tea is divided into green, black (called "red" in China), white, yellow, oolong, fermented (*pu'er*), and flower tea. Some of the most sought-after green teas are Longjing and Biluochun; among black teas, Keemun and Jinjunmei are special. National appreciation of good tea is on a par with the innate knowledge French people have of good wine and taken equally seriously.

In recent years, a different kind of tea hailing from Taiwan has become all the rage. Variously named bubble, boba, or pearl tea, after the chewy tapioca balls that people usually drink it with, this usually creamy creation can be drunk hot or iced, at varying levels sweetness, and with a dizzying variety of toppings, including pieces of fruit, grass jelly, and salted cream cheese.

Coffee is still less popular than tea, but there is a good variety of both well-known international chains and local coffeehouses in the larger cities. Starbucks' Shanghai Reserve roastery is the chain's second largest in the world and often has a line of people outside waiting to get in. If you go to smaller towns, you may want to bring your own.

China has a range of liquors unique to the country: on cold days try *huangjiu*, yellow rice wine, served hot in little porcelain cups and tasting rather like sherry. Its alcohol content is usually under 20 percent. More lethal is *baijiu,* China's answer to vodka and reportedly the most drunk liquor in the world. Its alcohol content can be anywhere from 40–60 percent. Moutai, the most prized brand of *baijiu*, is often drunk at state banquets and coveted by connoisseurs; the real deal starts from around US $145 (1,000 yuan) a bottle—if you find it for much less, it should probably be avoided. There are also many light Chinese beers, as well as a growing range of good Chinese wines, some produced in partnership with French wine producers.

SMOKING

Smoking is now prohibited in indoor public spaces, including restaurants, clubs, and bars. The law is not as strictly followed outside the major cities, where both patrons and owners may turn a blind eye to the ban. The same is true for taxis. Cigarettes are mostly very cheap, and though more than half of Chinese men are smokers, numbers are decreasing. On the other hand, while in the past it was socially unacceptable for women to smoke, it has become more common for them to do so.

SHOPPING FOR PLEASURE

Modern China is a shopper's paradise. Shops are open seven days a week, from about ten in the morning to ten at night, and sometimes even later. When Chinese tourists come to Europe, they complain about the limited opening hours of the shops they have come so far to patronize.

The Chinese love a good bargain, and though, in theory, shop prices are fixed, there is often room for a bit of haggling. In the markets prices start at about three times the eventual price you can expect to pay. If you can, bring a Chinese friend with you to play the bad cop. Traders can be very insistent and often know not only English, but also some Russian, French, and German. As China manufactures almost everything sold in Western shops, you can shop till you drop— and then buy an extra suitcase to bring it all home.

Many today prefer to shop online. China's e-commerce market already accounts for some 60 percent of all it's retail transactions, and exceeds that of the US, Germany, France, Japan, and the UK combined. There are a number of online shopping platforms worth exploring: Taobao, TMall, Jingdong, and seemingly endless stores on WeChat. The variety of goods, quality of customer service, and speed of delivery offered by China's online retailers are unmatched.

Fake Goods

In markets and small shops, everything with a logo is guaranteed to be fake; be especially wary of pirated CDs, DVDs, and computer software that may not work and will probably damage your device, or toys which may also be unsafe. Having said that, many goods of questionable authenticity, especially leather goods and apparel, can be of very good quality.

If you are offered anything "antique," it will either be a replica or else it is being offered for sale illegally. Genuine (you hope) antiques can only be bought at official stores and will bear a special seal authorizing their export. China has lost enough antiquities through war and conflict in the past and is hanging on to what it has left. You may find some legitimate antiques in Hong Kong, where they were taken by families fleeing the turmoil of the 1930s and '40s.

What To Buy

Apart from hi-tech products such as smartphones and computers, China is also rich in carving, embroidery, pottery and porcelain, glassware, weaving, printing, wood carving, and dyeing, and perfect replicas of ancient cultural relics. Folk art such as patchwork makes a good gift to take home. You can also find excellent silk, cashmere, pearls, leather goods, and home décor at a bargain. In major cities, there are specialized markets for each of the above. If you are staying longer, get some bespoke clothes made, especially formal and occasion wear. If you need something specific, with a bit of research you may find there is a whole street, or even town, dedicated to producing and selling that one item.

THE CASHLESS REVOLUTION

All cash transactions are in *renminbi* ("the people's currency")—also known as the yuan (dollar), a denomination of the renminbi currency—which is what you will be given when you change your money at the airport or at banks or hotels. There are 1, 5, 10, 20, 50, and 100 yuan notes. Yuan, which in spoken language is often casually referred to as "*kuai*"—piece, chunk—is broken down into 100 fen, and there are coins of 1, 2, 5, and 10. To complicate matters, the Chinese always refer to 10 fen as either a "*jiao*" or a "*mao*." So the Chinese would say two *mao*, rather than twenty fen, or five *mao*, rather than fifty fen, and so on.

Exchange rates are much the same everywhere and you can exchange money at banks, or your hotel. Keep in mind that according to current regulations, foreign nationals can only exchange up to US $500, or the equivalent in any currency, per day.

China is inching toward the time when the RMB becomes fully convertible; in the meantime, keep receipts as proof that your RMB were obtained legally so you can change the local currency back when you leave.

With all this in mind, paper money and coins have become a rare sight in daily life. China has been swept by a cashless revolution, and today most locals use mobile payment platforms, notably Alipay and WeChat Pay, for all their purchases. According to recent research, the average city-dweller carries less than 100 yuan (US $15) in cash, which is reportedly enough to last them about a month. People have been quick to adapt: some beggars helpfully provide QR codes for passersby to scan and transfer money directly into their accounts. No cash, no card, no phone? No problem! Some places are already experimenting with facial recognition payment.

CARRY CASH—OR NOT

As foreign credit and debit cards are frequently declined, when in China it is worth setting up an Alipay or WeChat Pay account that is linked to your bank account at home. From high-end restaurants to roadside fruit vendors, these platforms are accepted universally and are often preferred to cash or cards. Apple Pay is becoming more common but is not yet as widely accepted.

PARKS

Parks are wonderful places, the very essence of the collective spirit that is still so much a part of China. They are much more stylized than the open green spaces that Westerners are used to, with far fewer trees and more pavilions and rocks. Many retired people stay all day in parks chatting, giving their caged birds an airing, playing music from Peking Operas, or singing old songs. Ballroom dancing, Chinese chess (*xiangqi*), and card games are also popular. In some parks you will find "matchmaking corners," where elderly parents, concerned that their adult offspring are still single, will promote their child by way of a publicly displayed "résumé" that lists all the essential details, and network with other parents for potential matches. There are also sometimes "English corners," where Chinese students gather to practice their English in a group, sometimes with the help of a native speaker.

SPORTS AND EXERCISE

Go out at first light and you will find row upon row of
people silently absorbed in their morning exercises, each
going through the series of movements that make up
the slow, intricate ballet of tai chi (*taijiquan*) or *qigong*.
Qi means life force and *qigong* is a series of exercises—
combining movement, breathing, and visualization—
that direct the flow of energy around the body.

You can follow any sport in China as a player or a
spectator. Talking about sport is a good ice breaker:
most Chinese men and women are interested in sports,
especially those in which China excels such as basketball,
swimming, athletics, gymnastics, and badminton. The
most popular sports are those that do not need expensive
equipment, so although skiing, golf, and tennis are

increasingly enjoyed, far more people practice sports such as basketball (about 300 million play regularly) or ping pong. When the Beijing Olympics took place in 2008, millions volunteered to help the many visitors, some learning English especially, and China led the gold medal count.

Celebrity

One of the most famous Chinese sportsmen is Yao Ming, a basketball player who started playing for the Shanghai Sharks as a teenager and then finally played with the Houston Rockets. The only child of two basketball players, he stands 7 foot 6 inches (2.29 meters) high and weighed 11 pounds (5 kilos) when he was born. After injuries forced him to retire in 2011, he became an ambassador for endangered wildlife and donated much of the money he had made as a player to that cause, and to helping his old club, the Shanghai Sharks.

NIGHTLIFE

Once the sun goes down, the cities reveal a different face. While most larger cities boast bars and clubs that are on a par with those in London or Paris, it is Shanghai that earns the crown as China's nightlife capital. You will find the best clubs, bars, and restaurants here, some of which are consistently ranked among the best in the world. Karaoke bars, or KTVs are they are known, are also very popular; it is here that the Chinese shed their inhibitions and share their love of music. It is also probably the fastest way to bond with Chinese people, and the most fun. Many younger Chinese are big fans of *yexiao*, late-night dining, especially after singing the night away. Another popular night-time option is to go for a foot massage, which is both inexpensive and very relaxing. In small towns, entertainment options will be limited, but even there you'll find late-night outdoor barbecue stalls and the mandatory KTVs.

MUSIC

The love of music goes back thousands of years in China. Bamboo pipes tuned to resemble birdsong are thought to have been the earliest instruments played.

Musician Wang Xin Xin plays the traditional Fuijian *pipa*.

Confucius believed music to be a vital part of culture, and over succeeding dynasties Chinese musicians developed many different instruments, some such as the *guzheng*, unique to China, others such as the *pipa* coming from other parts of Asia. European music made its first known appearance in 1601, when the Italian Jesuit Matteo Ricci brought a harpsichord to the Ming court and trained four eunuchs to play it. Nowadays, traditional and modern Chinese and all forms of Western music happily coexist.

Chinese Opera

Chinese Opera has a number of regional variations, the best known of which are *jingju*, or Peking opera, and *kunqu*, which originates from the southeast region of

A performer of Sichaun's Bian Lian opera.

Jiangsu. Traditional drama involves acrobatics, fencing, and boxing, as well as music and singing. Singers wear elaborate costumes and highly stylized makeup; their audience, mostly older people, know the story by heart, so frequently get up and walk about during the performance, crunch noisily on snacks, and generally behave quite differently from the quasi-religious silence of opera audiences in the West.

Chinese Classical Music

The most atmospheric place to hear this is in teahouses, though concerts also take place in the big cities now that this type of music has been revived. Players often wear Tang dynasty dress; famous poems are set to music, sung in a thin falsetto voice, with eloquent pauses a part of the performance. It is not easy listening, and without financial support from the state would probably die out, but it is worth hearing.

Western Classical Music

The tradition of hard work, fierce competition, and perfectionism means that China produces many fine classical musicians, such as the world-renowned pianist Lang Lang. If you have a chance, go to a concert in one of China's stunning new concert halls, at much lower prices than you would pay in the West.

Revolutionary Songs

During the Cultural Revolution, these songs were the only ones allowed and for a while songs such as "The East Is Red" came to define mainland Chinese music.

The only place you are likely to hear them today is on souvenir electronic cigarette lighters emblazoned with Mao's face, and, much more pleasingly, in the parks, where older folk sing them with gusto, having apparently forgotten the suffering they endured when singing these songs was mandatory. That said, some of these old songs are very melodic.

Modern Music: Pop, Rock, and Rap

Pop, some from the mainland, some from Taiwan and Hong Kong, is by far the most popular genre in China. The country also has some real rock and rap gems. Young people listen to many of the same bands and singers as their peers in the West. Korean pop music, K-pop, is also very popular among young people, along with other Korean cultural exports, including fashion and television. Kugou and QQ Music are free and popular apps for discovering local artists.

Multiple music festivals are held across China. One of the most popular and longest running is the rock and alternative music Midi Festival, which takes place in Beijing. Another worth mentioning is the Great Wall Festival, both for its offering of electronic music and impressive location. Beijing is known for its vibrant indie music scene and excellent live houses, while Shanghai is the place to go if you're looking to catch a show by a major star, Chinese or otherwise. In any case, you may come across a real gem of an artist in a nondescript bar in any second- and third-tier city, as live performances are popular, and the singers are often very good.

ART

Classical Art Before 1949
Chinese painting is arguably the oldest continuous
artistic tradition in the world, quite unlike any Western
style of painting. Artists and calligraphers used brushes
dipped in black ink or colored pigments, applying
them rapidly to paper or silk. There are many subjects:
landscapes featuring mountains, rivers, and rocks,
scenes of court life, or animals. One of the most famous
is *Riverside Scene during Qingming*, painted by Zhang
Zeduan during the Song dynasty. It is on a scroll about
18 feet long and 10 inches wide (5.5 m by 25 cm) and
shows in fascinating detail the daily life of residents of
the city, with over 800 people pictured. Go and see it in
the Palace Museum in Beijing; the colors are still fresh
and bright, partly because these types of scrolls were
kept rolled up and only opened on special occasions.

Art After 1949
From 1949 onward, artists were told to imitate the Soviet
Union's style of socialist realism and some were tasked
with churning out the same pictures, for example of
happy peasants gathered around Mao, again and again.
In the late 1950s, giant outdoor murals of naïve peasant
art showing (idealized) rural life became popular. Many
priceless works of art—no one knows how many—were
deliberately destroyed by the Red Guards during the
Cultural Revolution as part of Mao's campaign against
the "Four Olds" (old customs, old culture, old habits,
old ideas).

Nowadays artists feel freer to innovate, but they still have to watch their step. Artist Ai Weiwei has become known worldwide for his original work, but his fierce criticism of the government has frequently landed him in serious trouble. As with religion, the government will only allow people to go so far.

After 2005, Chinese contemporary art had a major breakthrough in galleries and auctions around the world. Some of the most famous contemporary artists include Fang Lijun and Zhang Xiaogang, who are both known for their distinctive portraits

Chinese art, old and new, has been achieving record prices at auctions. Contemporary art spaces to visit and mingle with local artists, aficionados, and admirers include Beijing's 798 Art Zone or Shanghai's Moganshan Road Art District, both of which are spread across the complexes of old industrial buildings.

The Museum of Contemporary Art and Planning, Shenzen.

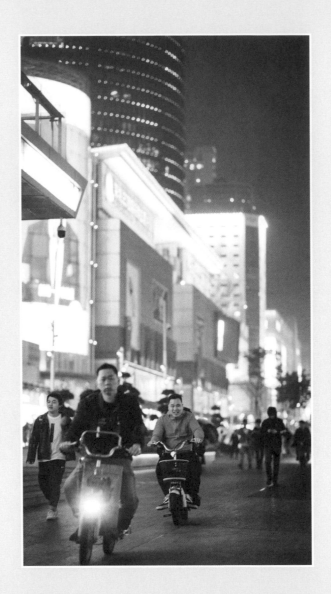

CHAPTER SEVEN

TRAVEL, HEALTH, & SAFETY

TRAVEL

The importance of moving goods and people has always been taken seriously by China's rulers. In the fifth century BCE the Chinese started building the Grand Canal from Beijing to Hangzhou—at 1,104 miles (1,176 km) it is still the longest in the world. By the tenth century they had worked out a system of locks to cope with differing heights of the land. In the past decades, China has poured money into its transport infrastructure, and while traveling in China is not always easy because of the huge numbers of people trying to do the same thing, its modern airports, high-speed trains, railway stations, and roads are impressive.

Safety records for trains, buses, and planes are fairly good and tickets are affordable. It is best to buy tickets in advance online, or use a travel agent. Two popular apps for travel deals include Qunar and Fliggy; however, they are in Chinese only, so you may have to ask your hotel staff or a Chinese friend for help. If you plan to travel between popular cities or at peak times, it is advisable to buy your tickets at least a few days in advance. For shorter distance journeys from the main cities, for example from Beijing to Tianjin, or Shanghai to Hangzhou, there are high-speed trains departing every few minutes and you can pick up your tickets from the station on the same day. Unless you are a masochist, do not travel during national holiday periods.

Travel in China, alone or in a group, is very safe. People may stare at you but are unlikely to molest you in any way; if you ask for help you will get it, but otherwise people will tend to leave you in peace. There will usually be someone kind and helpful, who will make it their job to adopt you temporarily, perhaps to practice their English or simply to make sure you are OK.

GETTING ABOUT TOWN

On Foot

Walking around towns can be difficult, due to the volume of people and traffic, but is never dull. Streets in China are packed with pedestrians, peddlers of everything from socks to pirated CDs to cell phone paraphernalia. Tiny homemade stalls offer food, bike or car repairs; tumbledown shacks housing family-run shops huddle in the shadow of huge designer outlets. The interest you feel in "people watching" will be reciprocated many times over by out-of-towners, who may stare at you openly. But their attention is good natured, and a friendly "*Ni hao*" (Hello) will be greeted with delight.

Walks in the countryside are best in the southwest, where there are mountains and bamboo forests to wander through; footpaths are marked and there are old Buddhist monasteries and ancient wayside inns to stay in.

Wheels

Thirty years ago, Chinese cities resounded to the ringing of bicycle bells as the entire population cycled to work or school; nowadays the background music is provided by millions of internal combustion engines and of motor horns sounded in cacophonous frustration. Car ownership in China has soared as people become wealthier; today there are more than 185 million privately owned vehicles on the road. Motorbikes, considered noisy and polluting, have been banned in many cities and largely replaced by electric bikes and scooters, which are affordable, fast, convenient, and, until recently, well tolerated by the government. Use of electric vehicles is becoming better regulated, and there is now a national speed limit of 15.5 miles (25 km) per hour, which some cities, like Beijing, have further reduced to 9 miles (15 km) per hour in a bid to curb the reckless habits of commuters and delivery drivers of running red lights and cutting onto the sidewalk— something to be aware of when walking the streets.

In poorer areas, people are still dependent on bicycles, tricycles, and antique tractors, often towing homemade trailers, loaded to gravity defying heights. They are used to transport everything from relatives, to farm animals, to precariously balanced piles of goods destined for sale in some faraway market.

Bike sharing, despite a dramatic scaling down in recent years, is still popular. Provider Mobike is the sole victor of a craze that, at its height, saw many sidewalks overrun with stationary bicycles as start-ups competed for riders and territory. Mobike's orange bicycles are everywhere, but their app will show the bike closest to you. Register with a small deposit, unlock the dockless bike by scanning the QR code, and go. Cars can also be rented, but you will need a driver as China does not recognize international or foreign licences. Obtaining a Chinese licence is possible, but it requires a generous amount of time and patience.

As part of China's fight against pollution, many older vehicles have been compulsorily scrapped and lie rusting in enormous scrapyards. Largely thanks to government incentives and preferential policies, China is now both the world's biggest producer and consumer of electric cars. In 2018, more electric cars were sold in China than in the rest of the world combined.

Public Transportation
Beijing and Shanghai both have excellent metro systems, which are user-friendly, cheap, quick, and reliable. Beijing's is the world's busiest, while Shanghai's, though still expanding, already holds the record for being the longest metro system in the world.

Urban buses are very cheap but also very crowded. In the big cities they tend to be modern and well equipped, with screens and electronic maps telling you (in English) where your stop is. Getting on is hard, and getting off can be harder, but people will make way for you and

Efforts to reduce congestion on Shanghai's roads means car owners may only use their vehicles every other day.

smile if you try and say "Excuse me" in Chinese, or even English.

Taxis

Taxis are easily hailed in the streets. They are strictly metered, though make sure that the driver starts the meter running. Few taxi drivers speak English, so it is advisable to get someone to write down your destination in Chinese and show it to the driver. The service can be gruff, the cars dated, and often in need of a good clean. Ride-hailing apps offer a more pleasant alternative: the most popular is Didi, which acquired Uber China and has an English-language option. Outside big cities, rickshaws are a pleasant way to travel, but agree the fare in advance.

Disabled Access

Facilities for disabled visitors are still not good, but attitudes toward those with disabilities are improving. Deng Pufang, one of the sons of Deng Xiaoping, was confined to a wheelchair after he "fell" from a window during the bitter power struggles of the Cultural Revolution. He devoted the rest of his life to campaigning for people with disabilities. There is still a long way to go: many streets resemble an obstacle race, with uneven sidewalks and no ramps. Disabled toilet facilities are rare. On a positive note, public transportation, especially the metro, is a lot more wheelchair-friendly, often more-so than in many Western countries, just because a lot of it is so new. There are plenty of Web sites for travelers with disabilities to consult before departure.

INTERCITY

Air Travel

Domestic air travel in China is very safe. The airlines expand their fleets at jaw-dropping rates, and most of the aircraft are very new. Three main airlines offering both domestic and international routes are China Southern Airlines, Asia's largest carrier, China Eastern Airlines, and Air China, although there are multiple smaller airlines too, and they all provide decent service. The air network is extensive, and airports are regularly upgraded. Buying air tickets online (on English-language Web sites) is straightforward and increased competition means there are some good deals to be found. The main issue with domestic air travel is that there tend to be a lot of delays, regardless of the airline. China's air space is largely controlled by the military and very little of it is open for civil aviation; on top of that, the huge number of flights to and from major airports means many flight paths are congested.

Rail Travel

China's modern high-speed train network is by far the world's largest and continues to grow at an impressive rate. With virtually no delays or cancellations, and reasonable ticket prices, high-speed trains are fast becoming the preferred method of intercity travel. You can travel from Shanghai to Beijing (745 miles, or 1,200 km) in four-and-a-half-hours in air-conditioned luxury, or from Beijing to Tianjin (71 miles, or 114 km) in half-an-hour, with

trains departing every 2–15 minutes. These high-speed trains are classed as "D "or "G" by the railway company. If you want to, or have to, experience the much slower, uncomfortable trains of China's recent past, they are still found in remoter regions and carry the label "K." China also boasts the fastest train in the world, the Shanghai Maglev, which runs at a dizzying speed of 255 mph (410 kph) from Shanghai to the airport at Pudong.

Book in advance and try to avoid traveling at Chinese New Year or during the national holidays in October when the whole country is on the move. Booking first-class is highly recommended if you want to enjoy more leg space and avoid loud neighbours, while in business class, leather seats can be converted into full-size beds. Get to the station early as there are security checks and lines can be long. While Chinese citizens can pick up their online-bought tickets from machines at the station, foreigners will need to go to the service counter, with a passport and booking number, to get theirs.

In the beautiful mountainous region of Sichuan and a few other far-flung outposts it was still possible to see a working steam train in 2019, but no one knows how long this will continue. There is an excellent railway museum outside Beijing.

Bus Travel

Long-distance bus travel has improved considerably and is popular for shorter intercity journeys. Tickets can be bought online or via agencies. There are on-board videos and music, but rarely an on-board toilet, and pit stops are few and far between. But there are advantages to bus travel. As novelist and long-term China resident, Nicholas Richards, wrote in *The China Dispatch*: "Bus travel . . . offers a gorgeous, leisurely ride . . . a taste of China that few other foreigners get to experience. Huge windows revealing luscious views of village life are just an arm's reach away, giving access to places that trains and planes wouldn't . . . take you, like the grasslands of rural Sichuan, or the mushroom fields of Yunnan. Best of all, you're sure to be the only *waiguoren* [foreigner] in sight."

Be Prepared

Public toilets are plentiful in large cities, and, since the government launched its "toilet revolution" in 2015, are a lot better now than they once were. In rural areas, however, open-pit latrines are still largely the norm and can be a challenge to the senses. Do not be surprised if going to the toilet is also a communal experience, with no doors to provide privacy. Toilets are also one place you will likely be unable to escape second-hand tobacco smoke. Take your own toilet paper and hand disinfectant to clean your hands, as there is rarely any available.

Travel by Boat

From four-day luxury cruises up the Yangtze River to short ferry hops with the locals around Hainan Island, Hong Kong, or Shanghai, China offers lovers of boat trips plenty of opportunity. There are many good private travel agencies who can help you find out more—ferry

Seven of the world's ten busiest shipping ports are in China, including the port of Hong Kong, pictured here.

companies are not yet as up-to-speed as airlines and trains when it comes to English-language Web sites.

RULES AND REGULATIONS

Visas

Individual travelers can obtain a thirty-day tourist visa at any Chinese consulate or other organization authorized by the Ministry of Foreign Affairs. Visitors wanting to stay beyond thirty days can usually gain an extension (up to sixty days) by applying to the local Public Security Bureau. The extension must be obtained prior to the expiry of the existing visa.

Business travelers require an invitation letter from a Chinese organization or enterprise to obtain a visa.

Some enter on a tourist visa, but this can lead to problems. You may wish to leave all the arrangements in the hands of an agency such as China Travel Service.

If you choose to handle your visa application yourself, check the latest requirements with your local Chinese consulate well in advance; even if you have been issued a Chinese visa before, requirements tend to change quite often.

Tibet

Tourists need to obtain entry permits from the Tibet Tourism Administration or one of its overseas offices. Try to travel there overland: if you fly in, you risk the fate of an American journalist who spent three days of his four-day Tibet visa (which he had waited months to obtain) in bed, recovering from severe altitude sickness. The body takes time to acclimatize to the thinner air of Lhasa, which is 11,975 feet (3,650 m) above sea level. Keep in mind also that traveling solo in Tibet is not permitted; you will need to join a group or at the very least rent a car with a driver.

Staying Within the Law

Holders of tourist visas must pass through Chinese ports of entry designated as open to visitors from abroad. Some places, particularly in border areas, are restricted, and travelers have been arrested, even expelled, for straying into these zones. Foreigners visiting China on normal travel permits should not engage in activities that do not comply with their visa,

such as taking up employment, study, or reporting; the
authorities are particularly sensitive about journalists
masquerading as tourists. Like many countries in
Asia, China has extremely strict anti-drug laws that
are enforced with heavy sentences, including capital
punishment.

Taking Photos
The Chinese have become selfie fanatics, so foreign
visitors snapping away in front of tourist sites just blend
into the crowd. But do not point your camera at soldiers
guarding government buildings, and be careful about
taking pictures at airports or anywhere that might be
considered "strategic," such as a dockyard or border post.

HEALTH

China's health care model is similar to that of the USA,
in that people must either pay for treatment or purchase
health insurance, which is topped up by the state. The
best medical care is available in large cities, where
private international hospitals and triple A-graded public
hospitals are available. The reputation of Chinese private
hospitals was heavily tarnished following a number
of public scandals in which patients were knowingly
misdiagnosed for financial gain. Their reputation is
improving again, however. Private international hospitals
provide excellent service but can often cost up to ten
times more than a public hospital. Triple A-graded
public hospitals employ the best medical staff, and there

is little doubt about their qualifications or experience. Bedside manner, however, often leaves rather a lot to be desired. As hospitals are inundated with patients, doctors can only allocate a few minutes for each and as such, there is no time for niceties. There is an extreme shortage of doctors in China overall, with only one GP for approximately every 6,500 people.

The government has been trying to address the growing disparity between rural and urban medical provision, and since 2005 around 800 million rural residents have been given basic medical cover, with about half of their costs covered by the government; around 95 percent of the total population now has basic health insurance. In rural areas, health care is rudimentary, with poorly trained medical personnel and little equipment or medication, though some areas have better quality care than others.

VACCINATIONS

Few are needed, but China does have a high incidence of hepatitis-B, with about one-third of the world's infections occurring there. In some areas inoculations against Japanese encephalitis are recommended. Rabies is present outside the big cities but rare in urban areas. Check online to see the full list, and get vaccinations done about two months before you go, as some take time to provide immunity.

If you become ill in China, call your insurance provider about the closest international hospital to go to. If, however, your insurance is limited, or you don't have any, take a taxi to the nearest public hospital (its address will be online in English) and ask to be treated in the so-called VIP department, or *guibin bu*. Most VIP departments have English-speaking doctors and nurses. VIP departments charge slightly higher prices but are still cheap by Western standards. If you need to go to an ordinary department in a public hospital, don't panic either. You may need to wait a while, but the doctors will be qualified, the younger ones will speak English, and it will be very affordable.

Going for dental care, cosmetic surgery, and other services in private clinics offer is not recommended unless you can be absolutely certain about the quality provided.

Air Quality

In cities, especially in the north, you may want to keep an eye on air quality, particularly if you are traveling with children or an elderly person. While most news outlets do report on air quality, a reliable app such as Air Matters, can be a valuable tool. Pollution levels can change in a matter of hours, and when they are high you should limit your time outdoors. Masks with air filters are common and available at most convenience stores.

HYGIENE AND PERSONAL SAFETY

When traveling you may consider taking your own chopsticks, cutlery, and cup, to be sure that you do not catch hepatitis-B from insanitary ones; in simple eateries, Chinese people will rinse cutlery with the hot water or tea that is provided as soon as they sit down. Chinese food is cooked fast, at high temperatures, and on the spot, so food poisoning is mercifully rare, but the use of dirty utensils, possibly washed in unclean water, is a risk. Largely due to the culture of food sharing, there is a prevalence of Helicobacter pylori bacterial infections, which can be avoided by the use of serving spoons and chopsticks when eating in a group. Road traffic accidents are an increasing hazard, and you should also check fire exits, which are frequently locked to keep out robbers.

Although China is generally very safe, you should be as careful as you would be at home. Watch out for pickpockets, especially in crowded spaces like the metro. Do keep a close eye on little children; there have unfortunately been instances of children having gone missing. Mostly, watch out for scams, such as the one where beautiful young women in the streets of Beijing and Shanghai ask gullible foreign men to take their photos, then invite them along to local bars for a drink and vanish, leaving the men with a huge bill or even the threat of violence. Con artists in China are famous for their creativity. If something doesn't feel right to you, trust your gut feeling. That said, violent crime is rare, and most Chinese will regard you as a guest in their country and take personal responsibility for your safety. If something does go wrong, report it to the nearest police station; for instance, if you have lost your passport, the police will issue a "confirmation of loss" report, with which you will be able to travel back home, if needed.

Your embassy can help in case of serious accidents, or the sudden death of a family member or friend.

BE PREPARED

- Don't even think about going to China without adequate travel insurance; make sure to have your insurance details and passport with you when you go to hospital. As most local hospitals don't have direct billing agreements with international insurers, you'll have to pay up front first and later make a claim to your insurer. Many hospitals also don't accept international cards, so you will either have set up a WeChat or Alipay account, or come with cash.

- Medicine from a reputable public hospital or international clinic will be reliable and safe. Medicines sold elsewhere may be fake, poorly stored, or out of date, so take with you a supply of any medicines you may need.

- Outside big cities and reputable hospitals, hypodermic needles may be used more than once, so take some unused sterile needles with you in case you need an injection.

- Take a spare pair of glasses, and your prescription.

- Keep all documentation related to any medical expenses you incur.

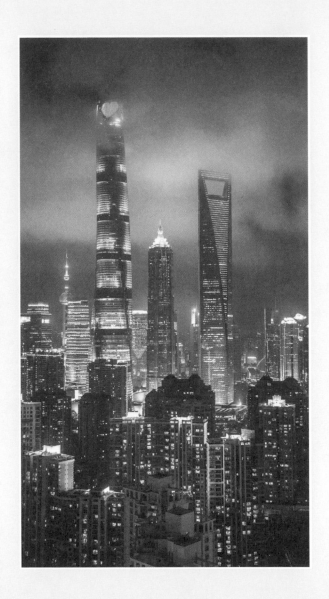

CHAPTER EIGHT

BUSINESS BRIEFING

Few tourists visit the Zhejiang Merchants Museum, set in the beautiful old town of Hangzhou, southeast of Shanghai. If they did, they would see an exhibition of portraits of twenty-first century local heroes: not soldiers, scientists, or revolutionaries, but successful entrepreneurs. Li Shufu, the boss of Chinese carmakers Geely, who acquired Volvo from Sweden is there; co-starring with him on the wall of fame are Ren Zhengfei, who set up Huawei, the telecommunications giant, and, most famous of all, the mercurial Jack Ma, founder of online retailer Alibaba. Homage is also paid to the first Chinese merchant, Fan Li, who some 2,500 years ago traded in Zhejiang province, and to a fellow Zhejiang resident born in the ninth century, Li Linde, the first known Chinese merchant to trade with Japan. Zhejiang province has neither natural resources nor good quality farmland, so its ingenious inhabitants have found other ways to scratch a living.

Where Zhejiang province led, others followed. Figures about China's growth are astonishing. Around

800 million people have been lifted out of dire poverty; there are some 60 million successful private businesses registered, including some of the world's biggest Internet companies. Jack Ma's company, Alibaba, sells more than e-Bay and Amazon combined. China has more than 300 billionaires, and McKinsey, the global consultancy firm, estimates that by 2022 China's middle class (that is, those with an annual income of between US $15,000 and US $34,000) will comprise some 550 million people, and make up 75 percent of urban households. To put things into perspective, this figure was at only 8 percent in 2010.

Doing business in China is getting easier. The World Bank's 2020 *Doing Business* report ranks China 31st out of 190 economies for ease of doing business, a major improvement from 90th place in 2015. The authorities have been working on reducing the notorious red tape and streamlining related processes.

Political interference in business is also a fact of life. Article 19 of China's company law states that a Party cell must be set up in every firm above a certain size, whether it is public or private. Professor William Kirby of Harvard Business School summarizes the "China miracle" as the Chinese people "opening their doors and finding other means to economic prosperity, by working around the barriers posed by the Party."

President Xi Jinping's government has been trying to move away from state investment in infrastructure toward growth driven by consumption and the service sector. These efforts have been complicated by a slowing economy and the US–China trade war; since

February 2018 both countries have imposed several rounds of tariffs on each other's imports.

Despite these difficulties, China remains one of the world's fastest growing economies. Its GDP growth in 2019 was 6.1 percent, in line with expectations and enough to land it on the list of top 20 fastest growing economies. The 2020 coronavirus pandemic saw a sharp downturn in GDP in the first quater, but confidence has returned as the economy steadily recovers.

THE NEXT DECADE

Investment in infrastructure may be down, but the service sector is growing in leaps and bounds: from education to entertainment, from health care to hairdressing, the rising middle class expects more and better, and both foreign and domestic firms are moving in to this market. According to the UK-based Institute of Export, consumers are "gradually shifting from luxury brand-led purchases to choices based on product quality, unique designs, individualism, leisure experience, and personal benefits." This shift has led to new business opportunities; among those listed on the Web site of the China–Britain Business Council are Chinese companies looking to import high-quality, safe products that their consumers can trust in the fields of baby care, food, beauty products, and many more, as well as Chinese firms seeking partnerships with overseas companies in areas ranging from music production to sports tourism.

BUSINESS PROTOCOL

The Chinese who deal with foreigners are well aware of China's attraction for potential business partners and are very knowledgeable about technology, pricing, and world markets. Everything will proceed at the pace of the hosts—which can feel very slow. You will not be able to do much to speed things along.

Your Visit

Arrangements for travel within the country will usually be taken care of by the organization you are visiting. You will probably be met by representatives of the organization when you arrive and be seen off by them when you leave. They will look after you well.

Seniority Matters

The Chinese are status conscious. When you are meeting a group of people, the most senior figure will often be introduced first. He or she may have an honorific but vague title such as President. However, the actual person with whom you proceed to negotiate may well be younger and probably more at ease with overseas visitors. It is important (though not always easy) to clarify just who is in charge. Your interpreter/fixer should be able to explain how the hierarchy works.

Greeting People

Shake hands with everyone in the group, starting with the most senior people. There is no custom of giving precedence to the female members of the group. The

Chinese incline their heads a little on meeting someone new, but there is none of the elaborate bowing that characterizes Japanese culture.

Business Cards

At a business meeting the first thing that happens is an exchange of business cards. Offer and accept cards with both hands (this also applies to gifts and anything given or received in a formal setting). When someone hands you a card, pause for a moment to read it—it would be considered rude to only glance at it before putting it away. At meetings, it is customary to keep the cards you have just received in front of you on the table. As exchanging cards happens often, take a large stock with you that include a Chinese version of your name, your company's name, and your job title on the back.

What to Wear

Smart casual dress is suitable for most industries, with the exceptions of banking or state owned enterprises, where a suit and tie is the norm. Women can be more flexible and creative in what they wear, but it is a good idea to remain within the limits of smart casual. Counterintuitively perhaps, the higher up the chain-of-command, the more casual the daily attire. Overall, the dress code will depend on the industry you are in. Banquets call for more formal wear, so take something extra smart, or go shopping locally— but remember that Chinese clothes sizes tend to be smaller than those in the West.

Time Keeping

Punctuality is considered very important in China, so it is best to arrive at meetings 5–10 minutes early. Being late will cause loss of face to your Chinese counterparts, especially if there is a senior person present. If you are late for whatever reason, make sure to let the Chinese party know as soon as possible.

Women in Business

The Chinese are equally happy to deal with both men and women. Women who visit the PRC on business report that they are well accepted by their male Chinese counterparts, and that it is not considered odd if they reciprocate toasts at banquets or take the lead in negotiations.

Communications

E-mail is not as popular as it is in the West. For both personal and business contacts, the Chinese prefer to stay in touch using WeChat, which is where you can expect far quicker response times.

NEGOTIATING

Meetings and Presentations

Chinese meetings tend to start off slowly. Initial meetings in particular are used to get to know the other party and to build a working relationship. A few talking points you could use as part of the warm up include: sharing positive experiences and observations

of your time in China; describing where you have been
and your personal highlights; asking your hosts about
their hometown (make sure to listen attentively to the
answer!); compliment Chinese food and mention your
favorite dish or cuisine. Sharing something about your
home country, discussing hobbies, and children are
also great ways to break the ice and to help build
familiarity. Trying to say a few words in Chinese will
also go down well.

Presentations should be in both Chinese and English,
with time allowed for translation. Bring your own
translator or a trusted Chinese-speaking partner. As part
of your preparations, make sure all materials used will
be available in Chinese as well. Come to meetings with
a clear set of objectives, which each side has had time to
think about, rather than using them as brainstorming
sessions. On the Chinese side, the most senior members
of the group will do the talking and it is considered rude
to interrupt. In more modern, go-ahead companies,
meetings will be less formal, with more of the lively give
and take that Westerners are used to. There is rarely a
written agenda (though hidden ones are common) and
things will move more slowly than Western executives
are used to.

When "Maybe" Means "No"

A Chinese person may feel that a direct "no" to a
request would be embarrassing and may try to convey
disagreement by evading the question or laughing. He or
she may have to consult their superiors or extract certain
concessions from you before answering. Phrases such as

"it is hard," "we need to think about it," "let's see," and the like usually mean "no." Quiet persistence and patience is the best way to play this.

Bribery

Requests for "commissions" (that is, bribes) are sadly common, but are likely to be made indirectly. Bribery is a dangerous game to get into; thousands of Chinese officials and business people have been arrested as part of the government's sweeping anti-corruption campaign. Foreign companies have been targeted too, such as the pharmaceuticals giant GSK, who were charged close to US $500 million for bribery.

Outcomes

Westerners tend to expect results from meetings. Chinese meetings, however, are an opportunity for people to get to know each other, build relationships, and state a negotiating position decided in advance. When negotiating, make sure to leave room between your starting offer and what you are willing to accept. Your Chinese counterparts will lose face if they feel they have been pushed into a corner—the aim should be to make any deal feel like a win-win.

Final Decisions Are Not Final

It can take a long time for a contract to be signed. The Chinese side may request changes to a contract even after it has been signed; get it translated into Chinese to speed things up. Remember, long-term relationships are considered more important than quick deals.

CHINESE/WESTERN BUSINESS COMMUNICATION STYLES

NAMES

Western: Tend to use first names on first meeting.

Chinese: Use titles such as Mr. or Miss, or Mayor, Manager, Professor. Use a person's English name once invited to do so.

HUMOR

Western: Tell jokes and use humor as an icebreaker.

Chinese: Little use of humor on first meeting—except for a carefully planned joke.

INTERRUPTIONS

Western: Feel free to interrupt the speaker and put their own point of view, but do not tend to use their phones during a meeting.

Chinese: Interrupting would be rude. Yet people take endless calls on their cell phones! Staff often pop in and whisper messages to senior executives. It is not seen as rude to whisper to a colleague while someone else is speaking.

MAKING SURE YOU ARE UNDERSTOOD

Western: It is usual to structure presentations and to recap what has been said. It is normal for the audience to ask for clarification if necessary. The speaker is to blame if something is not as clear as it should be.

Chinese: Being clearly understood is not a priority, perhaps because saying "I don't understand" is a possible loss of face, and because vagueness may be safer than being specific.

ARGUMENT VS. AGREEMENT

Western: People expect to argue things through; it is not rude to be adversarial.

Chinese: The Chinese can be quite argumentative among themselves, though a figure of central authority will not be questioned. Will close ranks in front of outsiders.

ATTENTION SPAN

Western: Short, and getting shorter. Westerners assume that people will be bored and try to come to the point quickly.

Chinese: Longer. The Chinese are trained from early childhood to listen politely and patiently. They do not come to the point quickly and you may not hear the information you have been waiting for until the meeting is almost over. The most important information will usually come last.

EYE CONTACT

Western: Too much eye contact makes people uneasy. Too little and they distrust you.

Chinese: Keep eye contact with your interlocutor. People who avoid eye contact are not considered trustworthy.

PRAISE

Western: Politeness and praise are important, but too much is seen as flattery and is mistrusted.

Chinese: Flattery is part of the negotiating process. It is given by praising people in front of their peers, and by expressing deference to superiors.

SELF DEPRECATION

Western: Used frequently in Britain, less so in the USA.

Chinese: Appearing humble and unassuming is a key value in Chinese culture and so individuals can be quite critical of themselves (though this may sometimes be a gambit to make themselves appear weaker). Individuals will rarely criticize their organization, or China.

GETTING THINGS DONE

Western: Orders and instructions are direct. They can be questioned.

Chinese: Orders are given more indirectly, but compliance is expected. Instructions are vague, yet carry authority.

ENTERTAINING: THE BANQUET

While almost every facet of life has changed in China over the last two decades, the style of a traditional banquet has altered little, though the anti-corruption campaign means less money is spent on them. Whether you are working, studying, or even just holidaying in China, you are likely to be entertained in this way at least once; if you are hoping to do business there, you will have to reciprocate.

The Good Guest

The timeslot for a banquet is usually from 6:00 p.m. to 9:00 p.m. Dress smartly; behavior will be surprisingly formal. Conversation will often be just between the most senior member of the Chinese organization and his or her counterpart on the Western side. Everyone else, more junior in rank, will tend to eat in silence or chat quietly, almost in whispers, among themselves, despite the Western visitor's well-meaning attempts to engage them. This is most marked at banquets with senior politicians, where sometimes the minister will do all the talking, while his retinue limit themselves to showing their appreciation of the conversation (or monologue).

Greetings and Gift Giving

Shake hands with everyone, in order of rank; this will be the order in which they are introduced. Exchange cards with people you have not met, using both hands to present your card. If you have brought gifts, leave the giving of them to the end of the meal. Significant gifts should not be given unexpectedly. Informing your hosts in advance means they will be ready to reciprocate and so will not be caused any loss of face.

Seating and Table Arrangements

The Chinese host, who usually sits facing the door, will place the most eminent guest in the seat of honor to his right, and the deputy Chinese host will place the next most senior guest on his or her right, at the opposite side of the table. The interpreter will probably sit to the right of the most important guest, with hosts and guests seated alternately around the table.

Be prepared to use chopsticks, though you can request a knife and fork. Most foreigners manage to persuade chopsticks to convey some food to their mouths; few master the knack of holding them properly, which Chinese children learn at their mother's knee. Asking for a demonstration from your hosts can be a good ice-breaker and cause much laughter. Banquets can consist of up to a dozen courses, so pace yourself. Taste a little of every dish or you will never make it to the end of the meal.

Do not be surprised if your host is continually placing the tastiest morsels on your plate—this is one way of honoring a guest, who should always wait to be urged to eat before helping himself. Watch what the Chinese diners do when they help themselves to the communal dish of food—they may use a serving spoon, "public chopsticks" (*gong kuai*) used by everyone to serve themselves, or their own chopsticks.

Lifting your bowl of soup or rice close to your mouth is not rude, and makes eating soup and rice less hazardous. There is a Chinese saying that after a good meal the tablecloth should look like a battlefield—so if you have made a mess of the area around your bowl, do not worry.

The Chinese do not, as a rule, eat dessert, although fresh fruit may be provided. Rice will be served near the end of the meal: it is seen as a "filler," in case guests are still hungry, and therefore it is polite to leave some in your bowl to show you have been well fed. Make sure not to leave your chopsticks upright in your rice bowl—it reminds the Chinese of incense burned as a tribute to the dead.

Toasts and Tea

Alcohol is used for toasts, but few Chinese are heavy drinkers. You will probably find three glasses beside your plate, one for beer, one for wine, and one for the more fiery *baijiu* (white liquor), which is distilled from sorghum and is up to 65 percent proof. The luxury brand Moutai is usually used for toasts, and you will often see the Chinese finish off a whole glass each time (but they are very small glasses). It is OK to use soft drinks or tea to toast with as well; the drinking etiquette at banquets that once resembled a competition to see who could get who under the table first is fast becoming a thing of the past.

Vegetarians may have a harder time of things than teetotallers; if you are vegetarian, warn your hosts in advance. If you only eat halal or kosher food, you may be out of luck, despite the history of Muslem influence in

China; however, there are restaurants in most cities run by people from Xinjiang province, so that might offer a solution.

Making Speeches and Proposing Toasts

Speeches, which end with one side toasting the other, usually take place soon after the beginning of the meal. The host will probably speak between the arrival of the first and second dishes, and the chief guest should reply a few minutes later, after the start of the second dish. Keep your speech short, appropriate, and follow it with a toast. Make a few appreciative comments about your visit, add some remarks about hopes for future cooperation, and avoid elaborate jokes as they are often untranslatable. If there are several tables, the host will at some point make a round of all of them, giving a short speech and toasting everyone at one table, then moving on to the next. During the toasting, everyone stands and only returns to their seats once the host has moved on.

Beware Jokes!

A Canadian journalist writes of how he was once at a banquet in the Great Hall of the People in Beijing. During the speeches, a visiting diplomat embarked upon a long and complicated joke in English. The poor Chinese interpreter, having tried in vain to translate it, finally despaired. He simply said, in Chinese, "The honored foreign visitor has just told a joke—please laugh!" The audience obliged.

Cheers!

At the end of the toast, the proposer says "*ganbei*" (literally, "dry glasses"), but caution is advisable because there will often be a number of toasts to follow. All-purpose "safe" toasts such as "To the friendship between our countries/companies/schools," are the order of the day, and normally people do not clink their glasses together. Guests may eventually propose slightly more original toasts, especially once they have downed a few glasses of Moutai. Do not pour your own drink; you will be taken care of by the waiters, or your hosts.

Making Conversation

Food, travel, families, and sport are good topics of conversation. Avoid talking about religion, bureaucracy, politics, or sex. Other safe topics include culture, and, of course, your business. Avoid serious business discussion though—social occasions such as these are for building friendships.

THE RETURN MATCH

If you decide to arrange a return banquet for your Chinese hosts before you leave, ask your interpreter, or whoever is organizing your visit, to help you. A table plan should be drawn up, and at a very formal banquet there should be place cards. As host it will be your job to keep plying your guests with food, and other people in your organization can do likewise to the person seated near them, especially each time a new dish arrives. Your guests will decline something offered to them several times before they feel able to accept, so you will have to keep pressing them to eat. Being the host or a guest at a Chinese banquet is a true cultural experience and, though not necessarily easy, can be very rewarding.

A Change of Style

When American President George W. Bush went to Beijing, Western rather than Chinese food was served at the welcoming banquet. As the banquet drew to a close, in place of the usual hasty farewells, an accordionist materialized on stage, and Bush's host, President Jiang Zemin, serenaded the Americans with a rendering of "O sole mio"!

WORKING IN CHINA

There are increasing numbers of foreigners working in China, and, while in the past the majority of positions available were confined to education, today opportunities exist in a far wider range of fields including IT, media, financing, manufacturing, and the service industry. For those interested in working in China, it is well advised to arrange employment before your arrival in the country as job hunting on a tourist or student visa will still require you to return to your home country to apply for the appropriate work visa.

China offers great opportunities for growth and career development, and many expats love the fast-paced lifestyle of China's megacities. Shanghai has repeatedly been voted the best Chinese city for expats. Life here is comfortable and the city incredibly vibrant. According to HSBC's Expat Explorer survey of 2018, Shanghai expats were also among the world's best-paid, with an average annual income of US $202,200. However, and this goes for anywhere in the country, unless you work for a foreign company, an international organization, or are high up the chain of-command at a major Chinese business, don't expect to earn a fortune.

It can be easy to get stuck in an expat bubble when living in China, but with a bit of effort to learn the language and acquaint yourself with locals, either through work or other social activities, your experience of integrating into Chinese society will be extremely rewarding and one that will remain with you for life.

CHAPTER NINE

COMMUNICATING

MANDARIN, CANTONESE, AND MORE

China's mountains and deserts have always made communications difficult, so it is not surprising that different forms of the language have developed. These are often referred to as "dialects," but since they are often mutually unintelligible, they may be thought of as separate languages. There are eight major variants of the Chinese language, including Mandarin, Cantonese, Shanghainese, Hakka, Amoy, Fuzhou, and Wenzhou, as well as minor regional variations. Mandarin is the official language used in both the PRC and Taiwan as the medium of education and is the common means of communication in China. In the PRC it is called *putonghua* (common or standard speech), as well as *hanyu* (the language of the Han people) and *zhongwen* (Chinese). In Taiwan it is known as *guoyu* or *huayu* (national language).

Chinese is a tonal language, part of the Sino-Tibetan family of languages. English, by contrast, belongs to the

Indo-European family. There are other South Asian
languages that work in the same way as Chinese:
Vietnamese, Burmese, and Thai, for example. Tonal
languages are those in which a variation in the pitch
of the voice conveys differences in meaning. For
example, *tang* said in a high, level tone means "soup,"
but *tang* said in a rising tone means "sugar"; *gou* said
in a fall-rise tone means "dog," but *gou* said with a
falling tone means "enough." There are four tones in
Mandarin. Cantonese has six. The four tones are:

level

rising

fall-rise

falling

Many Chinese words are made up of one syllable,
each represented by a single Chinese character.
Chinese has fewer sounds than some other languages;
as English has more sounds, there are few actual
Chinese sounds (as opposed to tones) that pose
problems for English speakers. Foreigners have
trouble even *hearing* the different tones, never mind
reproducing them. If you ask your Chinese contacts
to help you improve your pronunciation, you still
won't get it right, but your hosts can have a lot of fun
helping you. Any minor difficulty you may have in
learning some simple phrases will be far outweighed
by the positive reaction you will get from Chinese
people. The context, as well as the willingness of
your hosts to respond to your efforts, will aid your
understanding.

The Standard of English and Other Foreign Languages in China

The standard of spoken English in the cities is improving all the time; it is better taught, there are more native English speakers working in China, people travel more and there is (almost) unlimited access to English-language films, sitcoms, Web sites, books, and music. Plus, the motivation for learning English is greater than ever.

Few people speak other foreign languages, though some are growing in popularity, among them Japanese, Korean, French, German, and Spanish If you ever meet anyone who has studied any of these, he or she will most likely surprise you with an incredibly high level of fluency. Grammar is the biggest challenge for locals who study foreign languages; as difficult as Chinese characters are, they are not inflected in any way (meaning they always remain the same regardless of their function in a sentence) and so Chinese grammar is surprisingly simple—there are no tenses, genders, singular or plural forms, and certainly no cases. This is why these concepts are sometimes hard for Chinese speakers to grasp.

In the countryside, few will know English, never mind any other foreign language; rural schools have trouble recruiting and retaining teachers who can teach anything other than very basic subjects. When speaking English, remember to slow down, and if you are using an interpreter, remember to give him or her a chance to interpret a manageable amount before you move on to the next sentence.

Nowadays, many expats in China who do not speak Chinese will use translation tools to communicate with locals. WeChat messaging, for instance, has an in-built translation function. If you are translating between English and Chinese, Baidu Translate (Baidu Fanyi) also works very well.

Some Chinese, especially Cantonese speakers, tend to stress all English syllables equally, leading to a sort of machine-gun effect; combined with the fact that words like "please" are not used nearly as often in Chinese, this may lead to a perception of rudeness.

Pidgin English

The word "pidgin" (pronounced "pigeon," like the bird) comes from early Chinese attempts to pronounce the word "business." When traders from other countries first visited the coasts of China in the early 1800s they had no shared language. Pidgin English, consisting of a few hundred useful English words, filled this linguistic vacuum. The blend was enriched by a smattering of Hindi, brought over by traders from the East India Company. After 1949 pidgin died out; until then it was used as a way for foreigners and Chinese to communicate, as well as by speakers of different Chinese dialects to talk to each other.

Picturesque words from those days survive in stories such as *Tin Tin*, words like "*chop chop*," meaning hurry up. "*Chop*" on its own meant a trademark, or a name stamp on a contract. Another favorite is "*joss*" (as in joss-stick, a stick of incense), which comes from the Portuguese word *deos* (God); from this came the wonderful "*joss-pidgin-man*," or "God business man"—better known as a priest.

BODY LANGUAGE

Unlike in some of the more traditional societies in
Southeast Asia, the visitor to China does not have to
negotiate a minefield of possible ways of offending
their hosts. Years of compulsorily identifying with
the "workers, peasants, and soldiers" (that is, the
poorest classes of society) have made the Chinese
relatively relaxed about body language. So long as you
display ordinary good manners, that will be perfectly
acceptable.

One thing you are less likely to see than in the
West, and which you should not initiate, is kissing in
public; hugging and other exuberant "touchy-feely"
body language is still uncommon. This is changing
among the young urban classes, however.

There are a number of unique hand gestures for
counting that are based upon Chinese characters
and are worth being aware of. One to five is the
same as in the West, but from six things start to get
interesting: six is shown by folding the index, middle,
and ring fingers down into your palm, and extending
the thumb and pinkie finger in opposite directions;
seven is indicated by putting the tips of all five fingers
together; eight is shown by extending the thumb and
index fingers to form an "L"; nine is curling the index
finger up while other fingers are closed in a fist; and
finally, ten is shown by crossing the index fingers
of two hands together to form a cross sign. Zero is
a closed fist, although in some regions that can also
mean ten.

CHINESE CHARACTERS

Chinese is among the world's oldest written languages. It has no alphabet, but instead has around 50,000 characters (most of which have long fallen out of use, and whose meanings are a mystery to the Chinese themselves). Nowadays most Chinese people know between 3,000 to 8,000 characters. Many characters go back as far as the Shang dynasty, around 1200 BCE. Early Chinese writing was based on pictograms, which evolved into characters formed by a series of brushstrokes. Some characters still resemble pictograms: for example, the sun (*ri*) was a once a circle with a dot in the middle; now it is written like a box with a line across it. Water (*shui*) is three flowing lines; a person (*ren*) looks like a little headless human with two legs. Two characters can be combined to make a new one: "sun" plus "moon" make the character for

"bright." The character for "family" is formed by putting "roof" over "pig" (because rural families kept pigs, not because everyone disliked their family members).

Most characters consist of two parts: the radical, which shows to which class the word belongs and hints at its meaning, and the phonetic, which tells how it is pronounced. For example, the character for pure, or clear, *qing*, has two parts; the water radical and the part which gives the pronunciation, *qing*. There are about 250 radicals, some quite common, such as the one used for anything concerned with fire, others more unusual. Although learning characters appears a nightmarish task to Westerners, Chinese children start young and work hard at it. The literacy rate is 96.8 percent and a functional knowledge of between three and four thousand characters is enough for most people. On the mainland, in an attempt to raise literacy, Chinese characters underwent two rounds of simplification in the 1950s and 1960s. Traditional, or full-form, characters are still used in Hong Kong, Macau, Taiwan, and by the Chinese diaspora, they are much more complex.

PINYIN, OR HOW TO ROMANIZE CHINESE CHARACTERS

The modern system of transliteration, Pinyin, was developed by the PRC in the 1950s, replacing the older Wade–Giles system. It can be confusing to read books written some years ago with differently romanized versions of Chinese place-names, such as Soochow, now written Suzhou.

Pinyin is invaluable: telephone directories and dictionaries use it, and since Chinese does not have an alphabet, this is one useful way to organize information. Keypads use Pinyin: if you type in the word *ma*, using the two letters *m* and *a*, the screen gives you a choice of all the different Chinese characters that are pronounced "ma" (*ma* can mean mother, horse, and other things, depending on its tone and how it is written). You then choose the correct character.

Signs in public spaces are often in Pinyin and in English—even so, knowledge of at least a few Chinese characters is useful (exit, entrance, and so on), but not as vital as knowledge of the spoken language.

THE MEDIA

Censorship

All media in China are state controlled, and the Orwellian sounding SARFT (State Administration of Radio, Film, and Television) checks programs before broadcast. Journalists are often self-censoring for their own survival. Hard-hitting interviews with politicians are rare; news and current affairs broadcasts are prerecorded, rather than live, or with a ten-second delay. China received an extremely low ranking in the French organization Reporters Without Borders' 2019 annual media freedom index, 177 out of 180, a drop from previous years.

THE SOUNDS OF PINYIN.

Here is a written guide to the sounds of Pinyin. There are many apps that you can download to help you pronounce Chinese words correctly.

- **c** is pronounced as *ts* in "cats"
- **z** is pronounced as *ds* in "seeds"
- **q** is pronounced as *ch* in "cheap"
- **j** is pronounced as *j* in "jig"
- **x** is pronounced as something between *sh* in "shin" and *s*
- **s** as in "siesta"
- **r** is pronounced as a cross between *s* in "vision" and *r* in "red"
- **h** is pronounced as *ch* in Scottish "loch"
- **zh** is pronounced as *j* in "July"
- **a** is like *ar* in "far"
- **-ang** is like *ung* in Southern English "sung"
- **e** is like *er* in "her"
- **en** is like *en* in "stricken"
- **ei** is like *ay* in "hay"
- **ou** is like *ou* in "soul"
- **i** is like *ee* in "see," except after c,s,z,r, ch,sh, and zh, when it is like the *i* in American "sir"
- **u** is like *u* in "put"
- **ü** is like *e* in "see" but said with the lips rounded as if for "oo"
- **-ong** is like *ung* in German "Jung"
- **-ian** is like "yen"
- **ui** is like "way"

Foreign broadcasters such as CNN often have to pass their signal through a Chinese-controlled satellite so that transmission can be cut if sensitive topics or phrases, such as the Dalai Lama, are mentioned. However, the Internet allows people much more freedom to watch and listen to what they want, and satellite signal hacking systems can be bought for around 2,000 RMB (US $285) to access channels otherwise unobtainable.

TV and Radio

There are about 3,000 TV channels in China, and many local and national radio stations, some state run, some private, many available only online. TV and radio also broadcast in minority languages, such as Tibetan or Uyghur. CCTV is the state broadcaster, with foreign-language TV channels as well as 45 Chinese TV channels showing news, drama, music, and so on. TV used to have enormous audiences, but, just as in the West, these are fragmenting as there are so many other sources of entertainment.

Print

China has two main state-controlled news agencies, Xinhua and the China News Service. *Renmin Ribao* (*People's Daily*) is the government's official newspaper. Its English-language sister paper is *China Daily*, published in a print and an online version. Altogether, there are over 2,000 newspapers and 7,000 magazines, some state owned, many private, up from a mere forty-two in 1968—all Communist Party papers. In addition, around 25,000 printing houses and bookstores print and sell every genre imaginable: books are generally cheap and many Chinese are avid readers. Bookshops such as the huge one on Wangfujing, one of Beijing's main shopping streets, are crammed full of book-lovers of all ages, from children who can barely toddle to newly retired workers hungry for self-improvement.

CCTV headquaters, Beijing.

Reading in digital format is highly popular in China and it is far more common to see people scrolling through an entire book on their smartphones than it is to see them thumbing a paperback. Popular reading apps have made it convenient to read on the go; many charge per chapter or even for the number of words rather than per book. Internet novels (*wangluo xiaoshuo*) are extremely popular, often spanning tens of chapters and inspiring numerous spinoffs; many writers remain anonymous, others become celebrities.

SOCIAL MEDIA

Internet speeds in China are often faster than in Western countries, the devices used are newer and cheaper, and the Chinese have adopted social media with enthusiasm, for work, dating, shopping, planning nights out, booking tickets, and so on. Around 3,000 Western Internet sites are blocked—Google, Facebook, and YouTube among them; in fact, the only Western social network that can be easily accessed is LinkedIn. For the most part, though, the Chinese don't feel they are missing out, because China's own social media ecosystem is flourishing.

WeChat, which started as a messaging app, has evolved into an essential everyday tool that in 2019 was already boasting 900 million daily users in China alone. The super-app is now used to make video and voice calls, as a social media platform, to transfer money, to pay online and in bricks and mortar stores, to hail cabs, and to order food. Other novel functions include scheduling

doctor appointments, paying parking bills, and renting bicycles. If you haven't downloaded the app already, what are you waiting for?

Other popular apps include QQ, which is similar to Facebook, Weibo, the Chinese equivalent of Twitter, and Red, which combines online shopping with blogging and social media. Short video platforms, especially Douyin (or TikTok, as it's known in the West), are popular among young people. Because people are distrustful of information coming from official channels but still respectful of anyone who has managed to build authority for themselves, a wide range of influencers, locally known as KOLs (Key Opinion Leaders), enjoy much greater influence on Chinese social media than their counterparts do in the West.

Social media have had a huge impact on every aspect of life in China, not least on news reporting. For example, in July 2011 two high-speed trains collided near Wenzhou in Zhejiang province. Four railway carriages fell from the high-speed viaduct, forty people died, and more than a hundred were injured. In the West this would have been front-page news. But local officials panicked, brought the rescue operations to a premature conclusion, and ordered the railway carriages to be buried. However, "burying bad news" is a harder act to pull off now than in pre-Internet days. The online community found out what had happened and there was public outrage, at which point the normally cautious official media had to cover the story—a small victory for "citizen journalists."

SMARTPHONES

Smart Phone Penetration

When China first opened up to the world, it was quicker to take a taxi across town to talk to someone than to get through to them on the telephone. The residents of an entire apartment block might have shared one very poor quality phone line between them. As phones were used by so many people, they were thought to harbor germs, so people often covered the receiver with a handkerchief, making it even harder to hear what they were saying. At work, people tended to use the office phone to make all the calls they couldn't make from home—so no one could ever get through to workplaces either. Telephone directories were almost unknown, due to the obsession with secrecy: foreign embassies often had one, but kept it under lock and key. Now the Chinese are making up for lost time by talking incessantly everywhere they go on the latest smartphones. Approximately 70 percent of the country own their own smartphone, and with numerous domestic brands offering affordable handsets, the market will continue to grow. Domestic leaders include Huawei, Xiaomi, Oppo, Oneplus, and Vivo. Buying a Chinese SIM card is pretty straightforward—you can pick one up at any China Mobile or China Unicom store; just remember to take your passport with you.

MAIL AND EXPRESS DELIVERY

China Post's green and yellow post offices and delivery vans can be seen everywhere. Sending parcels and letters by surface mail takes time (a month from China to the UK is not unusual) but is cheap and reliable; airmail is quicker of course.

Express delivery services are cheap, reliable, and convenient. Items are picked up and can be delivered within the same day, if the two points are in the same city. Delivery to other destinations in China can usually be made within a few days. The most reputable companies for express delivery include SF Express, EMS, and ZTO Express.

CONCLUSION

The contradictions inherent in the Chinese pursuit of Western-style economic prosperity combined with tight political control were highlighted by former US Secretary of Treasury Henry Paulson in 2015, when he said: "It seems . . . incongruous to be, on the one hand, so committed to fostering more competition and market-driven flexibility in the economy, yet on the other hand, to be seeking more control in the political sphere, the media, and the Internet." These contradictions have not stopped China's economic growth powering the world economy for the past three decades, but now that it is slowing down, they may come home to roost. Mountains of unacknowledged debt may never be repaid, and structural reforms and more transparency are urgently needed.

Caught in the middle of the transition from a state-controlled, investment-led economy to a market-led one driven by the private sector are the ordinary Chinese, who, although they enjoy life more, constantly fear being left behind. Shanghai based writer, Mao Jian, describes the pressure felt by people governed by a new concept of "China Speed": "Got to speed up to make a buck. Tear down the old courtyard, fill in Suzhou Creek, register that domain name. One day late is forever late.

Longevity is no longer the goal; speed is the style in China today."

Where earlier generations were brought up to "Serve the People," and urged to emulate romanticized revolutionary heroes such as the penniless but perfect soldier and gentleman Lei Feng, nowadays China's role models are both real and rich. Foreign entrepreneurs such as Apple's founder Steve Jobs, and home-grown ones like Jack Ma, creator of the e-commerce giant Alibaba, are admired and imitated. Yet striving to succeed has arguably always been part of the Chinese character: many seem to be born entrepreneurs, willing to take risks, who work hard, save hard, and dream of getting rich. As the government retreats from managing its citizens' everyday lives, people are simply continuing the old traditions of relying on their own efforts and on strong family ties, combined with a new awareness of the wider world.

China's rulers run a tight ship, and foreign visitors should never underestimate the all-encompassing powers of what remains an authoritarian and sometimes unpredictable regime. You as a "foreign friend" may be simply there to marvel at the story so far, or privileged enough to play a part in the next chapter of the Chinese story. But over the decades that the writers of this book have been lucky enough to know the country, Chinese friends, colleagues, and students have continued to combine a mixture of warmth, loyalty, a ready sense of humor, a belief in the value of hard work, and a pride in their country's achievements, tempered with realism and the knowledge that there is still much to do. As UK-based Sinologist Martin Jaques puts it: "While possessed of the kind of inner confidence and experience that comes from being the heirs of a great civilization, the Chinese have no illusions about where they have got to and the tasks that lie ahead." Experts predict that China will have an even greater influence on the twenty-first century than it had on the twentieth; which is why time spent getting to know this fascinating country and its people will be an investment for life.

APPENDIX – SIMPLE VOCABULARY

Ni hao Hello (lit., you good)

Zao'an Good morning
(lit., peaceful morning)

Wan'an Good night (lit.,
peaceful evening)

Zaijian Goodbye
(lit., again see)

Xie xie Thank you

Bu keqi You're welcome
(in reply to thank you)
(lit., don't be polite)

Duibuqi Sorry,
(lit., I am unable to face you)

Bu hao yisi Excuse me
(before trying to pass, etc.)
(lit., I am embarrassed)

Qing Please

Qing wen Excuse me
(before a question)

Dui de Yes (lit., correct)

Shi de Yes (lit., it is so)

Bu shi No (lit., it is not so)

Bu yao No (refusing something)

Hao de Okay, good, fine

Qing zuo Please be seated

Qing gei wo Please give me

Qing jin Please come in

Yingguo England

Yingyu English (language)

Meiguo America

Jianada Canada

Aodaliya Australia

Zhongguo China

Zhongguoren Chinese man/
woman

Hanyu (in the PRC) Chinese
(language)

Wo bu hui shuo hanyu I can't
speak Chinese

Wo shi ... I am ...

Wo jiao ... My name is. . .
(lit., I am called)

Zai nar Where in . . .?

Canting Restaurant

Jiudian Hotel

Cesuo Toilet

Huoche zhan Railway station

Feijichang Airport

Mai Buy

Piao Ticket

Note: There are no direct
equivalents for "Yes," "No," or
"Please." For "Yes" you could
use *dui de*, which really means
"correct," or you can say *shi
de*, which means "it is so."
Instead of "No" you could use
bu shi ("it's not so"), *bu yao*
("don't want"—when refusing
the advances of overzealous
vendors, for example), or
bu dui ("incorrect").

FURTHER READING

Books, Fiction and Non-fiction

Ash, Alec. *Wish Lanterns: Young Lives in New China*. London: Picador, 2017.

Birkers, Robert. *Out of China: How the Chinese Ended the Era of Western Domination*. London: Penguin, 2018.

Chang, Jung. *Wild Swans: Three Daughters of China*. London: Flamingo (Harper Collins), 1993.

Chang, Jung and John Halliday. *Mao: The Unknown Story*. London: Jonathan Cape, 2005.

Hong Fincher, Leta. *Leftover Women: The Resurgence of Gender Inequality in China*. London: Zed Books, 2014.

Hua, Yu. *To Live*. New York: Anchor Books, 2013.

Kissinger, Henry. *On China*. New York: Penguin Press, reprinted 2012.

Ma, Jian. *China Dream*. London: Chatto & Windus, 2018.

Miller, Tom. *China's Asian Dream: Empire Building along the New Silk Road*. London: Zed Books, 2017.

Min, Anchee. *Empress Orchid*. London: Bloomsbury, 2004.

Qiu, Xiaolong. *Death of a Red Heroine*. New York: Soho Press, 2000.

Xinran. *Message from an Unknown Chinese Mother: Stories of Loss and Love*. London: Vintage, 2011.

Popular Chinese Web Sites and Apps

Alipay, a brainchild of Jack Ma's, is an essential mobile payment tool for many in China.

Baidu is the most popular search engine in China. You can also use it to download TV shows, music, and films. Copyright concerns do not appear to bother it overmuch.

Ctrip is great for booking flights, hotels, and package trips. It is available in many languages.

Dazhong Dianping (or simply **Dianping**) is a popular review website and app for restaurants, beauty salons, children's playgrounds, and a host of other businesses. It also offers group-buying deals.

Didi Chuxing is the main ride-hailing platform, and it offers a full English version.

Facebook is popular, particularly for news, shopping, and games. Its star is waning, though, as WeChat has taken over.

Meituan and **Eleme** are the biggest food delivery platforms; however, they are only available in Chinese. Sherpa provides hungry foreigners the same service in English.

QQ is an instant messaging service and offers a service similar to Facebook as well as news and music, shopping and games.

Taobao is the Chinese equivalent to Amazon—online shopping heaven.

JD is a popular online shop for genuine products.

Weibo is the Chinese answer to Twitter. Many users "follow" Chinese celebrities on Weibo.

WhatsOnWeibo.com is an English website for those who don't read Chinese but want to stay up to date with what's going on on Weibo.

Youku is the equivalent of YouTube for China, used for watching music videos, TV shows, and so on.

Other Web Sites and Apps

Chinadialogue.net is an independent and widely respected source of news and topical discussion about politics, the environment, and society in China today. The site is bilingual. SixthTone.com, RadiiChina.com, and InkStoneNews.com are all excellent sources on what's happening in China right now in terms of culture, innovation, and society.

PICTURE CREDITS

INDEX